LUCKY

THE WIT AND WISDOM OF GOVERNOR PHIL BATT

INTRODUCTION AND BATT INTERVIEW
BY ROD GRAMER

Essays from Governor C.L. "Butch" Otter, Governor Dirk Kempthorne, Lindy High, Marc Johnson, Randy Stapilus, Jim Weatherby

Caxton Press

ALSO BY ROD GRAMER

Fighting the Odds: The Life of Senator Frank Church (with Historian LeRoy Ashby)

The Good Assassin (a novel)

Lucky: The Wit and Wisdom of Governor Phil Batt
ISBN# 978-087004-642-1

First Edition

Library of Congress Control Number: 2021933041

Cover and book design by Jocelyn Robertson

Printed in the United States of America
CAXTON PRESS
Caldwell, Idaho

I dedicate this book to the Idahoans who work tirelessly to make Idaho Too Great for Hate.

– *Rod Gramer*

TABLE OF CONTENTS

LUCKY
THE WIT AND WISDOM OF GOVERNOR PHIL BATT

Governors Republican Phil Batt and Democrat Cecil Andrus – A unique political friendship. *Photo courtesy of Allan Ansell.*

INTRODUCTION
Rod Gramer

In 1985, while working on the biography of Senator Frank Church, I interviewed the historian David McCullough in Georgetown where he was living and researching a new book. I interviewed McCullough because he had written "The Path Between the Seas," the history of the Panama Canal. In the late 1970s, McCullough and Church had become friends while the Idaho senator was floor sponsor of the treaties that eventually turned control of the canal over to Panama, a prescient and courageous decision on Church's part that has preserved peace and commerce flowing for the past half century.

When we finished the interview, and the conversation turned to small talk, I asked McCullough what he was working on. He said he was writing a biography of President Harry S. Truman. I smiled and said that was nice. But the first thought that came to mind was, 'Who the heck wants to read a biography of Harry Truman?' But, as usual, McCullough had the foresight to write books which strike a nerve with readers at just the right time.

McCullough's "Truman" was published in June 1992 as voters were about to decide whether President George H.W. Bush or a new generation leader, William Jefferson Clinton, would be the next president. Dismayed at the shallowness of the campaign, McCullough wanted to get the Truman book out before the election. "I felt something needed to be said before people made a choice," he said later.

Weighing in at a hefty 1,120 pages, not only did McCullough's "Truman" connect with thousands of readers longing for something and someone authentic, but it went on to win the Pulitzer Prize for biography.

What McCullough understood at the time of our interview, and

I was too dim to see, was that Truman still had a lot to say to the American people even forty years after he left public life. "The book is about the country, not just about Harry Truman," McCullough said. "It's about who we are, and what we can be."

By now you may be asking: What does Harry Truman have to do with Idaho's former Governor Phil Batt? The answer is plenty.

Like Harry Truman, I think Idaho's 29th Governor has a lot to say, not just about himself and his political career, but also about what Idaho is and what Idaho can be. And, even though he has been out of public life for nearly a quarter century, Batt has a lot to say about who we are as Idahoans and the kind of people we can be.

I first met Phil Batt in 1974 when I was still a journalism student at the University of Idaho and was covering the Legislature with the incomparable Jay Shelledy of the *Lewiston Tribune*. Batt was already one of the most influential political leaders in the state. After finishing my degree, I went on to cover Batt as political editor of *The Idaho Statesman* and later as moderator of KTVB's public affairs show, *Viewpoint*. In 1994, I moderated one of the gubernatorial debates between Batt and Attorney General Larry Echohawk, a Democrat who was considered the front runner. On election night, Batt surprised everyone, including himself, by winning the election, just as Harry Truman did in 1948 over New York Governor Thomas Dewey. It was Batt's second run at becoming the state's chief executive, having narrowly lost the same race in 1982 to then-Governor John Evans.

In all the years that I have known and covered Batt, I always considered him Idaho's version of Harry Truman. Like the former president, Batt is short in stature for a politician, but always boxed above his weight. He answered questions in a straight-forward and clipped fashion. When Batt was on *Viewpoint*, I had to prepare twice as many questions as I did for other guests just to fill the thirty-minute program. And, like the piano-playing Truman, Batt is an accomplished musician, playing with the likes of the great Gene Harris and Chet Atkins. Even in his late 80s, I watched him wow the crowd at the annual Curtis Stigers concert to benefit the

Interfaith Sanctuary at the Egyptian Theatre. That night, Stigers proclaimed Batt his "favorite" Republican – something for decades many people, Republican, Democrat and Independent, would say.

Like Truman, Batt had a hair-trigger temper that could be launched suddenly at the most inconsequential slight. Once, when Batt was governor and I was executive news director at KTVB, my staff did a story on the evening news which Batt didn't like. That night he saw me across the room at a social event attended by many of the state's leading citizens. He made a beeline over to me and, in front of everyone, chewed me out good. But anyone who was on the receiving end of one of Batt's tirades, also knew that he would get over it quickly and the next day often apologize to the recipient of his ire. A friend of mine who was criticized by Governor Batt at a press conference told me that the following day the governor called him personally and asked him to stop by the Statehouse. In short order the chief executive of the state apologized and said, "I'm the governor of all the people in Idaho including you."

Not too many political leaders today admit they are wrong about anything, let alone personally apologize face-to-face with someone they think they wronged.

Batt shares other qualities with the former Democratic president. He cared about and battled for the underdog. He believed everyone deserved a "square deal." Batt still doesn't have tolerance when people are treated unfairly, especially those in the minority or exist on the margins of society. As a young man he quit his membership in the Elks Club when it rejected one of his closest friends because of his Japanese heritage.

And, like Truman, Batt's personal and political integrity was above reproach. There was never a hint of scandal in his personal or political life. When he could have taken unfair advantage of a political rival, he declined out of a sense of fair play.

Batt will be remembered most for three things. His unwavering support of human rights, for preventing the import of radioactive waste into Idaho, while cleaning up dangerous old waste, and his knack for finding common ground and even friendship with members of the opposite political party. He achieved this distinction while maintaining his own conservative Republican values of fiscal responsibility and small government. Batt never saw his political rivals as the enemy – only as people who held different political views from his.

At a time when the civil rights movement was not widely embraced, especially in conservative states like Idaho, Batt was the strongest – and often times lone – voice in the Legislature for giving all people equal opportunities for success in life. As a senator, he sponsored the legislation that created the Idaho Human Rights Commission. After years of legislators rejecting recognition of Martin Luther King's birthday, Batt eventually persuaded his Senate colleagues to pass a bill recognizing King's contribution to civil rights. In 1972, he supported passage of the Equal Rights Amendment, which would have outlawed discrimination against women, and in 1977, when Idaho repealed its ratification of the ERA, Batt was among the legislators who voted against its repeal.

Besides civil rights, Batt's other great accomplishment was negotiating an agreement with the federal government that required the removal of dangerous radioactive waste from what is now called the Idaho National Laboratory. Batt believed that without an agreement Idaho would lose the battle over waste in the courts. Purists like the movie star Bruce Willis denounced the agreement because they didn't think it went far enough. Even Batt's close political friend, former Governor Cecil Andrus, criticized the agreement at first, but later supported it. Believing he had negotiated the best deal possible Batt went to the people to decide whether he or Bruce Willis was right, thus putting his nascent governorship on the line. In the end, the voters overwhelmingly affirmed their support of the agreement, giving Batt a vote of confidence. Then for nearly thirty years Batt and Andrus teamed up to defend the agreement when the federal government dragged its feet on satisfying the terms of the deal or wanted to bring new waste into the state.

But the interview I did with Batt for "Lucky" isn't just about the past – it's also about the present state of affairs in our national and state politics. Even at the ripe old age of 94, Batt speaks with a clarity, honesty and authenticity rarely found in the current generation of political leaders. He bemoans the lack of civility in our politics. He wonders why there is not more compromise to get things done. He is disappointed that few, if any, leaders of either political party do anything about the national debt we are leaving to our children and grandchildren. He questions why today's leaders, especially in his own party, do not outlaw discrimination on the basis of sexual orientation. He asks why Idaho's legislators for so long denied basic health care to thousands of their fellow citizens. He's grumpy that policymakers do not invest in the infrastructure so basic to the safety of our citizens and the flow of our commerce.

Batt is also self-deprecating, gives credit where credit is due, lights up when talking about two of his favorite things, music, and animals, and is sincerely honest about when others were right, and he was wrong, while never making excuses or blaming anyone. He speaks warmly about the people who helped make him the person he is, especially his mother who was the first to teach him about treating all people with respect and his Uncle P.G. Batt who tutored him about business and about how to treat his employees like friends.

In short, the voice that comes through the conversation I had with Batt is one that long-time Idahoans will be familiar with and new citizens to our state will find refreshingly honest.

It is no wonder that in 2019 Batt was given the Idaho Medal of Achievement, the highest honor any Idahoan can receive. Typically, Batt was overwhelmed with gratitude for receiving the award, but also wondered with typical humility why, as a politician, he should receive it over non-politicians who were more deserving in his mind.

As I write this, it occurs to me that Phil Batt is the last of a generation of leaders who shaped the best parts of Idaho we have today. Gone are most of Batt's contemporaries. Gone are nearly all of the lawmakers who served with Batt in the 1965 Idaho Legislature, widely considered the greatest session in Idaho history. Gone is Democratic Governor John Evans, his political rival and yet someone he respected for his contributions to Idaho. Gone is Senator James McClure who played a critical role in negotiating Batt's nuclear waste agreement. Gone is Cecil Andrus, the Democrat with whom Batt is often associated with because of their unique political friendship, dogged effort to remove radioactive waste from Idaho, and because of the way they both carried themselves when they disagreed.

Batt and Andrus. They were the odd couple of Idaho politics. One was a tall drink of water, the other short. One's words were so spare you would have thought they were silver dollars. The other could mesmerize listeners with stories about his hunting exploits. One was from the northern woods of Clearwater County, the other from the southern flatlands of Canyon County. But they also shared many qualities. Both had a great, and often self-deprecating, sense of humor. They both put integrity over expediency. They both loved Idaho and its people. They both used the levers of power for the people, not for their own personal gain.

For full transparency, when I first envisioned this book, I thought it would be a joint interview with Governor Batt and Governor Andrus. I wanted to ask them what they thought about the current political climate in our country. I wanted to know what they thought we could do to bring civility and decency back to our politics. In short, I wanted to ask them how our current crop of politicians could better emulate their leadership style. Unfortunately, Governor Andrus died in August 2017 before I could tackle this project. For a while, I gave up on the book idea. Then I thought, no, Governor Andrus is gone, and we miss his voice greatly, but Governor Batt still has a lot to say to the people of Idaho.

For my money, Batt and Andrus provide a model for how politics should be practiced, not as a war of mutual destruction so dominant in our current politics, but as a noble calling that can solve the real problems people face, making the world just a little bit better for everyone. And I hope that belief which was the underpinning for this book comes through in my conversation with Governor Batt.

My interviews with Governor Batt took place in three sessions in the winters of 2019 and 2020 at his modest home in Boise. The third session took place the day after Governor Batt's 93rd birthday on March 4 – the day we celebrate as "Idaho Day." When I asked if it was just a coincidence that he was born on the day Idaho became a Territory or that it was a sign he was destined to become governor, he just giggled and smiled. In all we talked for three hours as he sat on the couch in his family room, his beloved golden retriever, Sully, at his feet. Over the next several months we refined the questions and answers in a format that you see in this book. As you can imagine, at his age Governor's Batt's physical health has declined, but his mind is still sharp. His answers were still straight-forward, his words clipped and efficient. In other words, in this conversation you will find the same old Phil Batt.

Unfortunately, you won't see in our interview any mention of the COVID-19 pandemic or anything about the 2020 presidential election, or Joe Biden's victory, or the storming of the U.S. Capitol on January 6, 2021. That's because shortly after our last meeting the virus struck Idaho with a vengeance and it was simply unsafe for me to visit Governor Batt. I still wonder what he would have to say about these events.

I also asked a few people that Batt knew well and who worked with him at various times in his political career to write essays about their experiences with the governor. Governors C.L. "Butch" Otter and Dirk Kempthorne, and Lindy High, a long-time Batt aide, all generously contributed essays for this book. In the spirit of the bipartisanship Governor Batt always practiced, I also asked my old friend, Marc Johnson, to write an essay. Like me, Marc covered Governor Batt as a journalist for many years and later served as Governor Andrus' chief of staff. Marc is a perfect person to reflect on the friendship between these two old political war horses. I also asked long-time Idaho political observer and author Randy Stapilus to reflect on his recollections of Governor Batt. And I am honored that Jim Weatherby, the dean of Idaho political scientists, agreed to write about his memories of the governor. I owe all these long-time friends and associates a debt of gratitude for contributing to this project.

Reading both my conversation with governor Batt and these essays you will see that we are even making some news. For example, Governor Batt predicted in our February 2019 interview that after he died the state would renegotiate his agreement with the INL. He was wrong. Governor Little renegotiated that agreement eight months later while Governor Batt was very much alive. Governor Kempthorne writes about how a surprise visit at his home from then-Governor Batt finalized his decision to give up his U.S. Senate seat and return to Idaho and run for governor. Governor Otter relates how Batt was the person who got him into politics. In the pages of this book, you will find other interesting political tidbits not previously reported as far as I know. I don't mean for this book to be a scholarly project – just a conversation with one of Idaho's most influential political figures and the reflections of prominent people who know him.

As I write this our nation has a new president whose immediate challenge is to end a deadly pandemic and to help our economy rebound from one of the worst economic downturns in American history, one which still has millions of Americans out of work. Our new president also has other challenges to face, growing income inequality, systemic racism, and climate change, just to name a few. Today we need authentic, empathetic, and effective leadership more than ever – the kind of leadership Phil Batt brought to our great state.

Many people probably wonder if the kind of leadership Phil Batt embodied is even possible from today's leaders. Whether we can ever go back to the days when politicians found common ground and worked together for the betterment of our people. Whether gridlock, ruthlessness and unbridled partisanship is a curse we just have to live with.

But I'd like to think that those days are not left to the dustbin of history. That, as Abraham Lincoln said at another divisive and dark time, that we can be "touched by the better angels" of our nature. That politics can, once again, be a noble and authentic calling focused on the common good, not on personal promotion and self-aggrandizement.

In closing, I'd like to paraphrase David McCullough. This book isn't just about Phil Batt. It's about who we are as Idahoans and Americans. And, most importantly, it is about who we can become as a people.

ROD GRAMER was a long-time newspaper and broadcast journalist. He served as political editor and editorial page editor of *The Idaho Statesman*. He was executive news director of KTVB in Boise where he also moderated the *Viewpoint* public affairs show for ten years. He is the co-author of "Fighting the Odds, the Life of Senator Frank Church," and a novel, "The Good Assassin." For the last several years he has served as president and CEO of Idaho Business for Education, a non-profit working to help strengthen the education system in Idaho.

Photo courtesy of Idaho Business for Education.

INTERVIEW
Governor Phil Batt with Rod Gramer

The following conversation with former governor Phil Batt took place over several months, starting in the winter of 2019 and ending the day after his ninety-third birthday on March 4, 2020 – coincidentally, the day Idahoans celebrate as "Idaho Day." Three of the interviews took place at his home in Boise and were recorded. In other cases, Governor Batt responded to written questions. The conversation below was arranged to flow in a way that would maximize the experience for the reader. Minor edits to both the questions and answers were made for clarity, but the meaning and substance of questions and answers were not changed. For the recorded interviews, Governor Batt was casually dressed and sat on the sofa in his family room, with his beloved golden retriever, Sully, resting at his feet. Unfortunately, shortly after the second interview Sully passed away, and was sorely missed when the third interview was conducted.

RG: You once said that you have been called many things—the Little Giant, Squeaky, Machine Gun—because of your rapid-fire responses. But you say the name you think is most appropriate is Lucky Phil. Why do you think you have been so lucky?

GOVERNOR BATT: Well, I was presented with a lot of opportunities in my day. I've had some disappointments, so has everybody else, but I was given plenty of opportunities in politics, business, and other things. And I took advantage of those. I call myself lucky in that, for sure.

RG: You were born and raised on a farm in Canyon County.

GOVERNOR BATT: Three miles from Wilder. [1]

RG: You came of age during the Great Depression and World War II. How did those years shape both your personal and your political views?

GOVERNOR BATT: Well, I've always been sympathetic with Republicans. I think they're far the better associates. But all the national politics is so bad I can't identify with either one of them (political parties), really.

RG: You cannot identify with either party now?

GOVERNOR BATT: Yeah. Well, I'm still Republican, but there's a lot of bad things that happen in the Republican Party also. I'm a Republican, and I don't mind identifying myself as a Republican, always. But a lot of the things in national politics, I don't identify with either party.

RG: What are some of the things you don't like which are happening nationally?

GOVERNOR BATT: Well, in the first place, nobody worries about our debt, which is going to eat us alive. It's $21 trillion or more. One of the Democratic candidates (for president) just announced a couple of days ago. She talked about it. Nobody talks about it. We're going to have to face up to it. I'm going to be long gone, thank goodness. But our national politicians don't seem to care that we go further in debt, take on more responsibilities. They're not responsibilities, they're things that they wish they had. So, they just promote their own deals and keep spending more and more and forming new reasons to have federal intervention on our life. I think it's a real mistake on everybody's part, but, you know, being one of the members (in Congress) back there, what could you do? You couldn't get anywhere, really.

RG: What do you think the members of Congress should do?

GOVERNOR BATT: Well, they should provide bipartisan policy. Decide that they must do something about the debt. They have to cut a lot of the things out. Most of them were not necessary to begin with, a lot of them, that is. They need to get together and trim a lot of it off.

RG: Republicans used to talk a lot about the debt, but not so much these days.

GOVERNOR BATT: That's right.

RG: When you were growing up, the Democrats, even here in Idaho, controlled the White House and Congress. Yet, you joined the Republican Party. Why?

GOVERNOR BATT: Well, my dad was strictly a free enterpriser, and my mother, too. I wouldn't discuss politics with her, but she's the one who caused me to be more versed in human rights. FDR got us through the war and did a very good job of it, but the programs that he brought forward, a lot of them are no good. They're not necessary. I was an Eisenhower man.

ON HIS MOTHER

RG: You say that your mother had a huge impact on you when it came to human rights. What do you mean?

GOVERNOR BATT: Well, yes. I shared religion with her. She was way more important to my life in everything except business. She was wanting the best for everybody. She wanted people to make their own lives better.

RG: I understand that during the Great Depression, when unemployed men came to your house, asking for food or a chance to work, that your mother gave them food.

GOVERNOR BATT: Yeah. I remember, as a kid, seeing how poor people were and how much they wanted work. My dad was good at trying to give them a chance. He hired a black man. The only one I ever saw. He gave him a job. Nobody else would.

RG: Clearly, your mother had a huge influence on your life.

GOVERNOR BATT: Yes. I was the fifth of five children, and I think she spoiled me more than the rest of them because I was her youngest, and I was three-and-a-half years behind my brother. She taught me how to play and how to play music. We were close in the church. I attended a church with her and quite a bit later, too, the First Baptist Church. She was very religious. I think she expected me to treat everybody right.

RG: That is where the value of treating people fairly came from?

GOVERNOR BATT: Yes, I think so.

RG: What else do you remember about your mother?

GOVERNOR BATT: I remember when I shot a little bluebird with my BB gun. I was pretty proud of that, so I showed it to her. And she thought I ought to feel sorry for that bird. I kind of regretted having killed that bird, but I did.

RG: Sounds like she had a great heart.

GOVERNOR BATT: Yeah, she did

RG: Was your mother the one who instilled a love of music in you?

GOVERNOR BATT: Oh, yes. She sure helped a lot in my music. She was a piano player. All the kids took to music. Got it into all of them, except my brother John. But we all liked music.

ON HIS FATHER

RG: Tell me about your father.

GOVERNOR BATT: Well, my father taught me how to work and how to make some money. He was a good man. He didn't have much to do with other people, and he just worked.

RG: In your memoir you wrote about wanting to return to the University of Idaho after the war to finish your education. But your father discouraged you from doing that.

GOVERNOR BATT: Yes, he did. I think he only had about three or four grades himself, but he was smart.

ON HIS UNCLE PERCY GEORGE BATT

RG: What influence did your uncle, Percy George Batt, have on your life?

GOVERNOR BATT: He was a great mentor of mine. My dad was more of just, "Get on the farm and work." P.G. owned the little place that I bought, and that was my office. P.G. would call me to sit down and discuss things for hours. He was just a great influence on me and a good influence in general. He built everybody up, always. And ran a packing shed and made a lot of money on it.

RG: How did he mentor you?

GOVERNOR BATT: Well, he was a great Republican himself. We talked about how people want to carry on business and respect their employees. He was very close to his employees, as I was later. He taught me how to do that, really. P. G. taught me a lot about being a good employer. He taught me to appreciate the value of the employees and to reward them with decent wages and close friendships.

ON THE GREAT DEPRESSION

RG: I want to ask you about an incident that happened when you were a boy. There was a farmworker who worked on your family's farm. You and some other boys harassed him. You got into a dirt clod fight with him. He eventually lost his job. You wrote that you felt badly about doing that.

GOVERNOR BATT: Yeah, I felt really bad about that.

RG: Was it a learning experience for you as a young boy?

GOVERNOR BATT: Yeah, a little bit. Dang kids. You know, we did everything. Throwing clods at somebody was not unusual.

RG: I understand some gypsies showed up at your farm to work during the Great Depression.

GOVERNOR BATT: Yeah. They camped out at our headquarters. It was just a tool shed at the time. They camped out there, and they put on a big show for us all the time. They liked to dress as gypsies while they worked, too. I can't remember how good of workers they were, but they sure had a good time. And I liked them a lot. [2]

RG: And they sang in the fields?

GOVERNOR BATT: Yes, they did.

RG: That must have appealed to you.

GOVERNOR BATT: Yes, it did. Jamaicans (who also came to work on the farm) just sang a little in the field, but the gypsies did more.

RG: It is amazing that in the Great Depression all these people with diverse backgrounds from around the world came to work in Idaho.

GOVERNOR BATT: Yes.

RG: You also recalled how during World War II, when male labor was scarce, Mexican farm workers arrived in Idaho for the first time.

GOVERNOR BATT: Yeah, they came as single people for a while. We had a place built for them in the labor camp. They were just great workers. [3]

RG: The single men came first and later they brought their families up from Mexico?

GOVERNOR BATT: Right. And we didn't sponsor them, necessarily, after that. We were sponsoring them at first. Then we finally built our labor camp more modern. They're still using it. But they were good houses.

ON HIS START IN POLITICS

RG: In 1964, your brother, John, decided not to run for re-election to the legislature. Apparently, you had just a mild interest in politics, but decided to run for the legislature. Why?

GOVERNOR BATT: We were scared of the communists. A lot of people were at that time. And we banded together to see how we could diminish their influence. They selected one person for each office to run for—the mayor of Wilder, state representative, Canyon County representative. In fact, I think we had about half a dozen, or maybe eight, people running for office. They all got elected. My brother, John, didn't like the legislature at all. He hated to make those compromises. He would not do it, so he just decided one term was enough for him. I thought it was a pretty fascinating thing, and I gave it a shot myself. It worked. [4]

RG: Cecil Andrus used to say that education was the reason he ran for the legislature. He didn't feel the state was doing enough in education. Was there a big issue that got you to run for the legislature?

GOVERNOR BATT: I can't remember what issues we had. But I was elected as majority leader in my first term in the House and then I moved to the Senate and was elected pro tem.

RG: You moved up into leadership fast. Why do you think you got elected majority leader and then pro tem so quickly?

GOVERNOR BATT: Well, reapportionment. A lot of people weren't all that qualified in legislature, and they didn't really care about it. So those of us who entered in later were interested in how the legislature worked. We wanted to be part of it. All my friends were involved also.

RG: You once recalled how Senator Art "Pop" Murphy helped you get acclimated to the legislature. Sounds like he was a big influence on you, even though he was a Democrat.

GOVERNOR BATT: Yes. I was a pro tem. He wanted to train me on senate rules. On many days we would show up early and he would show me things about the rules. He also prayed for me. I needed it.

RG: Pop Murphy prayed for you every day?

GOVERNOR BATT: Yes. He was quite a religious guy.

RG: Did it help you?

GOVERNOR BATT: Yeah, I thought so.

RG: It sounds like he was a real mentor for you in the legislature.

GOVERNOR BATT: Pops Murphy was sixty-eight years old in 1967 when I moved to the Senate, where I became majority leader. I was always early to the chamber and Pops was already there. He took me aside and led a short prayer with me. We seldom missed that ritual. He said it was okay to have fun but that I should respect all members. I loved learning and practicing the rules and he was my complete instructor, often giving me a thorough grading on my knowledge and performance. I became very accomplished and I was fast. Perry Swisher said I was the best in recent history. I wrote a poem about Pops Murphy in my book.

My contacts with all members regardless of party were useful to both me and them. It was always pleasant to talk with Cecil before and after the session. Pops always approved of the congeniality with all members. We did a good job and were proud of it.

ON THE 1965 LEGISLATURE

RG: You served your first term in the 1965 legislature, which many people regard as the greatest legislative session in Idaho history. There was judicial and reapportionment reform. That legislature passed the first sales tax, which has been used ever since to help support education and other government programs. Why was the 1965 session so productive?

GOVERNOR BATT: We were forced into solving the issue of reapportionment. We had to compromise to make it work. [5]

RG: Did you support adoption of the sales tax?

GOVERNOR BATT: By all means.

RG: Why?

GOVERNOR BATT: Mainly to support education.

RG: There is a movement right now to repeal the sales tax on food. Several candidates campaigned on doing that in the 2018 election. What do you think of that idea?

GOVERNOR BATT: There are good arguments on both sides of it, but I had never even considered taking it off groceries. Where would they get the rest of the money (to support state services)?

ON HIS LOSING 1982 CAMPAIGN FOR GOVERNOR

RG: You lost the 1982 election to the incumbent, John Evans, by less than one percent of the vote. During that campaign you said that we would need to increase the sales tax to prevent cuts in education. How did that affect the outcome?

GOVERNOR BATT: John would say that we didn't have to add anything to the sales taxes, and I knew he was wrong. I debated him on that and put it part of my platform. But John, once he got elected, increased the sales tax. I knew he'd have to. He was totally wrong. I think he fooled himself into thinking it was okay. But John was a good man, basically. [6]

RG: Do you think that issue cost you the election?

GOVERNOR BATT: The Democrats were running the deal (state) at that time, and I had a good campaign. And I darn near won, but it was because I had a good campaign and knew what I was doing. It was hard to knock the Democrats out.

RG: What about that Big John comic book at the end of the campaign? The one that portrayed John Evans as a pawn of the union bosses. How did that affect the election?

GOVERNOR BATT: Yeah, it was a mistake, and I didn't publish it. Somebody else did.

RG: Did you try and stop it from being distributed?

GOVERNOR BATT: Yeah.

RG: But they would not listen to you?

GOVERNOR BATT: Well, in some cases, you've got to have dirty campaigns, but no use to having one then. There was no way to prove that he was doing bad things.

RG: Do you remember who was behind that?

GOVERNOR BATT: I think probably Ralph Smeed and other Canyon County supporters.

RG: But you believe it hurt your chance of winning the election?

GOVERNOR BATT: Oh, I think so. Well, I know it did.

RG: When you lost that election, did you ever think you might run for governor again?

GOVERNOR BATT: I didn't think about it. I didn't plan to, that's for sure. But I ran a good campaign.

ON CHAIRING THE IDAHO REPUBLICAN PARTY

RG: In 1990, eight years after you lost that race, Cecil Andrus had been re-elected to an unprecedented fourth term, both seats in Congress were held by Democrats, Larry LaRocco and Richard Stallings, and the Idaho Senate was tied 21-21. So, you decided to run for chair of the Republican Party. Why?

GOVERNOR BATT: Well, I thought we could make a big improvement. I went organizing into every county. We had meetings of Republicans in every county. And we had a good reason for saying we should get more Republicans, and it was very successful. [7]

RG: Was organizing every county the key to your success in ultimately electing more Republicans?

GOVERNOR BATT: I think so.

RG: Why do you think the Republicans had lost their way by 1990 when they had been the dominant party in Idaho for most of the state's history?

GOVERNOR BATT: Well, Cecil Andrus was very popular.

RG: So, you rebuilt the Republican Party county by county?

GOVERNOR BATT: Well, we did it by the book. We got prominent people representing the party, by far better than the Democrats.

RG: You mean you had better candidates?

GOVERNOR BATT: Yeah, our candidates were very good, and the Democrats were lazy, I think, at that point, a little bit.

ON HIS 1994 CAMPAIGN FOR GOVERNOR

RG: In 1992, as chair of the Republican Party, you started looking around for someone to run for governor in 1994?

GOVERNOR BATT: Yeah. [8]

RG: Who were some of the people you thought should run?

GOVERNOR BATT: Butch was one. Dirk Kempthorne was another. In looking them over, I thought I was by far the best candidate.

RG: In 1992, Dirk Kempthorne ran for the Senate and won. That took him out of the running for 1994.

GOVERNOR BATT: Yeah. Right.

RG: You didn't expect to win that 1994 election, did you? Why do you think you defeated Idaho's Democratic Attorney General Larry Echohawk?

GOVERNOR BATT: During the 1994 race, Echohawk attracted most of the early support. Larry had national and local publicity.

He was favored by about thirty percent more voters than I was on the first poll taken. I predicted he would win. He was rude to me during my campaign and showed up challenging me (on the front steps of the statehouse) during my own group planning the rest of my campaign. Mr. Echohawk insisted on being able to speak to my group, and that cost him criticism.

ON THE NUCLEAR WASTE ISSUE AT IDAHO NATIONAL LABORATORY

RG: The biggest issue you faced when you were elected governor in 1994 was the dispute over the federal government bringing nuclear waste into Idaho, and the radioactive waste already stored at the Idaho National Laboratory. That was an issue that Governor Andrus had raised during his administration, even blocking a shipment of waste on the Idaho border by putting a state police car on the railroad tracks. Tell me what you were thinking when you became governor and were confronted with the nuclear waste issue. [9]

GOVERNOR BATT: Well, I knew that we were going to have to get some kind of compromise worked out. The navy would've sued us, and we would have lost. No doubt about it. So, they (navy) would've been free to do whatever they wanted then.

RG: So, you thought negotiating an agreement and finding common ground was better than taking your chances in court?

GOVERNOR BATT: Right. The nuclear waste thing was tough for me. Gov. Andrus had his stomach full of promises and lack of action on the part of the federal government. I didn't appreciate the fact that he physically blocked the shipment of spent naval fuel into Idaho a few days before he left office.

The naval authorities said they only had a few days to move the spent fuel before impacting normal activities. I chose to negotiate a big cleanup plan, and INL was willing. Governor Andrus decided to stay out of it. He finally helped in the agreement after Senator McClure, Clive Strong and others helped me put it together. Governor Andrus was the hero in the public and I was the goat, but he gave me praise—except for a little dig in his book. [10]

He (Governor Andrus) never prepared me for that terrible jolt I got in taking on that terrible assignment.

RG: You and Governor Andrus never talked about the nuclear waste issue after you were elected and before you took the oath as governor?

GOVERNOR BATT: No.

I didn't think it was a fair criticism in his book when he said I should have got more payment for failure to meet deadlines. He was wrong. I got the best deal I could get.

You know, Cecil came around totally with it. He started out . . . well, he criticized me in his book for not negotiating enough money through the contract. But he thought finally that our negotiation was just about right.

Cecil and I together forced the government to toe the line and effect much needed cleanup. My agreement severely limited our obligation to handle nuclear waste. My successors have the power to change the agreement. There will be changes good or bad sometime in the future.

Andrus and I hung together in demanding strict compliance, much to the benefit of Idaho. The agreement has been a good thing for Idaho. Parts of it have not been completed. Andrus and I came out on the same page. No damage was done to our friendship. [11]

RG: Do you remember what Senator McClure did behind the scenes to help you?

GOVERNOR BATT: He'd give me his sense of what may be negotiable, and what we could live with.

RG: So, Senator McClure played go-between between you and the Department of Defense?

GOVERNOR BATT: Yeah. He must've had the ear of the navy people.

RG: Who else helped you with the negotiations?

GOVERNOR BATT: Clive Strong (Idaho deputy attorney general) was one. He was very instrumental.

RG: There was a critical meeting in Minneapolis where you met with an admiral. At that meeting it looked like you had hit a stalemate, and you were about to walk away from the negotiations. But eventually you had a breakthrough. What happened?

GOVERNOR BATT: I gave them my own tale of woe. I mean, how important it was that we got something done. But I think McClure was better at putting that together than anybody. Pretty good.

RG: But you also played a key role, right? Because you were dogged about trying to get an agreement that would benefit Idaho?

GOVERNOR BATT: Oh, no question about it. It (INEEL) was just a dumping ground over there. Terrible thing.

RG: The nuclear waste agreement ultimately went to a vote of the people.

GOVERNOR BATT: I would like to talk about that. Nobody was for it, leaving it the way it was. I mean, Bruce Willis's humbugs were wanting to put me to work as a grocery clerk. But, you know, he (Willis) was totally against the navy or anybody putting any stuff on our soil. But the other folks, they didn't want it either. Very few folks at that time really wanted to have the navy or the people go ahead and dump things there. I just did that (won the referendum) mainly with persuasion.

RG: Were you surprised the voters supported you?

GOVERNOR BATT: No, I was working hard at it. I think the best thing I did was telling them (Idahoans) what it meant to them. And that it was far better to pass it (the agreement) than to leave it alone.

RG: You had faith that the people of Idaho would support you on this issue?

GOVERNOR BATT: Right.

RG: You and Governor Andrus have spent the last several years defending that agreement and holding the federal government accountable for keeping its end of the bargain.

GOVERNOR BATT: That's right. I stuck with Cecil on that.

RG: Why did you and Governor Andrus do that?

GOVERNOR BATT: Part of the agreement said that, unless we carried out the terms of the agreement, that we would not get any manufactured nuclear waste as long as the agreement had some parts that weren't fulfilled, and we have never had that done. The high-level liquid waste is a very difficult one. They've not figured out how to do it. So, we're still in a position of saying that they didn't fulfill their part of the agreement.

They've been proposing various ways to put some experiments in INL that involved new commercial waste, which is totally against the agreement. They're trying to get that changed by the governor and the attorney general. They're the ones that can do it.

RG: The federal government wants to renegotiate the agreement?

GOVERNOR BATT: Yes.

RG: And you want them to live up to the original deal?

GOVERNOR BATT: I don't want any new nuclear waste put in here.

RG: You and Governor Andrus have had to stand up to a lot of powerful people the last few years.

GOVERNOR BATT: I'm satisfied they (will) do that once I'm dead.

RG: Are you saying you think Idaho's leaders will renegotiate the agreement and allow new waste in after you are dead?

GOVERNOR BATT: There's some good reasons why INL wants some material or some new projects to work on. We used all our people to clean it up. Now we've got too many people, but they're smart people and well-paid. So, the Idaho Falls Chamber of Commerce, and other people, want us to get some new projects, and maybe that's the thing that they'll do. I don't know.

RG: Do you really think that they will open the doors to more waste when you're gone?

GOVERNOR BATT: I do. I've talked to Brad (Little) and Butch (Otter) and everybody. They all want to do it. [11]

RG: Do you think people of Idaho will stand for that?

GOVERNOR BATT: Well, I don't know. At one time, they were all excited about not doing things like that, but you don't hear them (the people) talking about waste leaking into the Snake River and all that stuff like you used to.

RG: That's because you had an agreement to stop nuclear waste from entering the state and getting the remaining nuclear waste cleaned up.

GOVERNOR BATT: Yeah.

RG: Now that Governor Andrus is dead, will it be more difficult for you to defend the agreement alone?

GOVERNOR BATT: Well, I'll make the same statement again. I'm sticking up for what I had with Andrus.

RG: Are you satisfied that they've done all they can to clean up the waste?

GOVERNOR BATT: No. We got the high-level liquid waste. Plus, a lot of the manufactured stuff almost operable in New Mexico. They broke down in there, and they haven't got that fixed yet. They've got about half of that stuff to send out yet, all part of the agreement.

RG: As long as you are around will you keep fighting to have the waste removed?

GOVERNOR BATT: Well, I got no choice. I doubt that there's going to be a tough resistance again. I still think people are so excited about it, and they like to see Idaho Falls get some new stuff.

RG: It sounds like you're a bit fatalistic about waste coming back into Idaho once you are gone.

GOVERNOR BATT: I think so.

ON NOT RUNNING FOR A SECOND TERM

RG: Why didn't you run for a second term as governor?

GOVERNOR BATT: I was more popular than I ever was at that point, so I would've got it (re-elected), I think. In fact, some of them ran a survey and said I could get eighty percent at some point. [12]

RG: Given that, why didn't you run again?

GOVERNOR BATT: Well, my wife wasn't too fond of it, and I wasn't so fond myself. I mean, I practiced term limits on myself all the time I was in there. I never ran more than six years at one point. I thought politicians should not be career people, and I still think that.

RG: You just thought four years was enough?

GOVERNOR BATT: Yeah. I had practiced term limits in all my political career, although I feel people would have welcomed me to run again. I have mixed feeling about term limits. But I wanted to have them for myself.

RG: Were there other things in life you wanted to do?

GOVERNOR BATT: I had all kinds of opportunities, and I still had at the time I got out of there. I never did much traveling or having any fun and wanted to do some of that. I had a little airplane. That was good.

RG: Did you enjoy being governor?

GOVERNOR BATT: I did. Most of it, yeah. In fact, I enjoyed it, really.

RG: Was it a better job than you thought it would be?

GOVERNOR BATT: Yes. It was a good system where you could get things going in the legislature and get the executives behind it. I thought that's the way the thing ought to work. We did that, mostly. It was very good.

RG: What are the most important characteristics for a governor to have?

GOVERNOR BATT: In my opinion, a governor should try to save the taxpayers' money. He or she should promote fewer laws and regulations. The people can run their own affairs in most cases better than the government can.

ON HUMAN RIGHTS

RG: You have always been a champion of human rights. Why?

GOVERNOR BATT: My position on human rights is healthy and heartfelt and had nothing to do with the political parties.

RG: How did you come to adopt your views on human rights?

GOVERNOR BATT: I learned to respect human rights from my mother. I first saw the terrible injustices when I joined the air force in World War II. I was in basic training in Biloxi, Mississippi. I saw Blacks forced off the sidewalk to let Whites go by. Separate toilets. Separate drinking fountains. Blacks forced to the back of the bus. Just totally unacceptable, but most of the people didn't think it was. I thought that was totally unfair. People carried on their prejudices. Most people did. I mean, it wasn't a rare thing. When I saw some injustices happening, I didn't like it. It did make an impression on me.

In my farming I had a preponderance of Mexican employees—either U.S. or Mexican citizens. I saw the signs—"No Mexicans allowed." We all saw raw abuse of human rights. A lot of it has been corrected—more needs to be done.

RG: Later, after you returned to Idaho from the service, you made the decision to drop out of the Elks Club. Tell me about that decision.

GOVERNOR BATT: One of my best friends was a Japanese feller, Kay Inouye. Very good friend of mine, and I tried to get him into the Elks. They wouldn't take him because he was Japanese. He was a really good man. And (the club) just turned it right down. So, I wrote them a letter, said I was dropping.

RG: Did they change their policy because you dropped out?

GOVERNOR BATT: No. As a matter of fact, I got a lot of criticism from some other folks. But, no, I never tried to join again.

RG: You once said Idaho is being unfairly portrayed as an anti-human rights state.

GOVERNOR BATT: Well, I don't know why I should've said that, but I did.

RG: Do you still feel we are unfairly portrayed?

GOVERNOR BATT: The legislature still won't pass a thing to accept gays for gay marriage. It's against the law (in Idaho) . . . Of course, it's covered in the national deal (by the United States Supreme Court decision upholding gay marriage).

RG: So, you think it hurts our image in other parts of the country when we don't provide those kinds of civil rights?

GOVERNOR BATT: Yes, it does.

RG: As a journalist who watched you in the legislature and as governor it seemed to me that you always had a sense of fairness about people, especially people who were not being treated equally.

GOVERNOR BATT: Well, like I said, my mother influenced me a lot in that. She believed in everybody getting treated equally, not unequal. Be aware that people had certain rights of their own that we didn't just trample on.

RG: Back in the 1960s, when you were championing the Idaho Human Rights Commission and the first Idaho Civil Rights bill, that probably wasn't very popular with some people.

GOVERNOR BATT: Yeah. I carried on my own hearings for fifty days. I had people come in and tell me what their problems were. I think I convinced most of the legislators that we should get a human rights commission.

RG: You did that to create a fairer playing field?

GOVERNOR BATT: Yeah. I mean, there were prejudices within the public that were tolerated. In fact, they were backed by the law, so we needed to change the law. That's what we did.

RG: You also fought to have the state recognize Martin Luther King's birthday. It took a while. Idaho was one of the last states to recognize his birthday.

GOVERNOR BATT: Wonderful man (referring to Martin Luther King). He just said what he thought. He was brave about it, but he wasn't trying to stir anybody up. Good man. Of course, he got assassinated.

RG: Looking back on your political career, would you say that your fight for human rights was one of the most important things you accomplished?

GOVERNOR BATT: It was important. It was perhaps my greatest legacy.

ON SUPPORTING FARM WORKER RIGHTS

RG: Another thing you fought for in the legislature was toilet facilities for farm workers. The legislature wouldn't pass that for a long time, but you finally got a bill through.

GOVERNOR BATT: Yeah. But, in addition to that, for forty years prior to my legislative service I carried workers' comp (for his farmworkers). You know, if somebody had a little something wrong with their hand, they could go to the doctor and get it fixed up on my workers' comp. But other people wouldn't do that. There are very hideous wounds or accidents on a farm. Of course, the employer probably felt some obligation and did what they could, but there was no requirement to do that. [13]

RG: You finally got workers compensation for farmworkers passed when you were governor. Did you lose friends over that issue?

GOVERNOR BATT: I don't know how many, but some.

RG: How did you convince legislators it was the right thing to do?

GOVERNOR BATT: That's one of the few things I did some cranking on. I got people in my office and talked to them about it. Nobody had a good reason not to. I mean, it cost a lot of money, but it wasn't bad. And once we got it in, we were able to reduce the cost considerably. [14]

RG: Because more farmers were paying into the fund?

GOVERNOR BATT: Yeah. Other professions always had it. Why should a farmworker have to put up with injurious practices when nobody else had to do it?

ON EQUALITY FOR WOMEN

RG: This winter there was a dinner where each of the former governors were asked to give some advice to newly-elected governor Brad Little. When it was your turn to comment, you simply said, "Listen to the women."

GOVERNOR BATT: Women have made their presence a lot better felt than in the earlier days, and it's been a proper thing or a useful thing for our country. Men in power have to listen to the women. They give some good advice.

RG: Women got the right to vote one hundred years ago. But in Idaho they got the right to vote in 1896—almost twenty-five years before the rest of the country.

GOVERNOR BATT: Yeah, we've been pretty good in some respects. I had a majority of women working for me in the governor's office. We had a great staff. I've always championed equal rights for everyone.

ON "ADDING THE WORDS" FOR LGBT RIGHTS

RG: Let me ask you about a current hot civil rights issue. Maybe you follow the "Add the Words" debate we've had in the legislature. Now, it's not against the law to discriminate against gay, lesbian, and transgender people. Backers of "Add the Words" want to put in code a prohibition against discriminating against those people. Do you think it's a good idea?

GOVERNOR BATT: Yes, I've backed it for years.

RG: Why have you supported it?

GOVERNOR BATT: Well, to put it in our code that we cannot discriminate against anybody, for any reason. It's mainly about the homosexuals. Well, I've got a great deal of sympathy with them. They should not be discriminated against.

ON THE EXPANSION OF MEDICAID

RG: Health care is a big issue nationally right now. Here in Idaho, voters just approved expanding Medicaid to thousands of Idahoans who fell into the so-called gap—they make too much money to qualify for Medicaid, but too little to afford health care. What did you think about that initiative? [15]

GOVERNOR BATT: I voted with them to put it in. In fact, I would've put it in previously because other states have done it and taken in a lot of (federal) money, whereas Idaho could have. I'm not sure we've been wise to let it go this long.

RG: Why did you support the expansion?

GOVERNOR BATT: Well, the federal government was sending ninety percent of the funding which is very helpful to Idaho. There were also some people being left out with their income. I'm not a good student on it. I don't know who they are and how bad off they are, but they presented a pretty strong case to put some people on it. (They) would not get on it otherwise.

RG: There are an estimated 90,000 Idahoans who now qualify for Medicaid.

GOVERNOR BATT: It seems to me there could have been reasonable compromises that could take place without going the way (by initiative) we did.

ON THE IMMIGRATION DEBATE

RG: What do you think about current debate over immigration?

GOVERNOR BATT: I think we should treat Mexico and Canada as the well-deserved neighbors that they are. However, our border situation with Mexico is broken and unsustainable. It's important that we welcome economic health and security to the U. S.

RG: What do you think about what is going on today regarding the refugees at the Mexican border? President Trump wants to build a wall on the border. Are you discouraged that we are having such a big debate over whether to have immigrants or not have immigrants?

GOVERNOR BATT: I'm discouraged with the whole argument.

The Democrats, for instance, now think they want border security, but they won't say how to do it. They won't cooperate. And Republicans on the other end, represented by President Trump, do not put out a lot of cooperation either. You know, everything in the national Congress, they just automatically oppose each other.

ON DONALD TRUMP'S WALL

RG: Do you think we should build Donald Trump's wall from San Diego to the Gulf of Mexico?

GOVERNOR BATT: Well, there has to be some discussion about it. It's not needed in some places, and it's needed very badly in other places. I can't see why they can't compromise, talk about it. Get some sensible ways to put some impediments in there, but they argue about what the word "wall" means. I think they're foolish to not argue that out.

ON THE DREAMERS

RG: What about the dreamers, those who were brought into the country illegally when they were children by their parents? There are about 300,000 of them here in the country now. The United States is the only country they've known. What do you think we should do?

GOVERNOR BATT: We've got to work that out and put them in here.

RG: You mean give them citizenship or allow them to stay in the country legally? Is that what you'd do?

GOVERNOR BATT: I would think citizenship.

RG: What should we do with people who are attempting to come into the country illegally or have entered the country illegally?

GOVERNOR BATT: Oh, I think we have every right to close that border to people that will not apply legally to come in.

ON THE ASYLUM SEEKERS

RG: And what if they do come and ask for asylum in our country because they have been persecuted for their political beliefs or fear that their life or a family member's life is being threatened?

GOVERNOR BATT: Well, your own Christian faith wants to prevent them from being prosecuted in their own country. But that all has to be worked out and argued out. I'd like to see the Democrats and Republicans both get more cooperative in that and other parts of immigration.

ON PRESIDENT TRUMP'S NATIONAL EMERGENCY DECLARATION

RG: Are you aware that President Trump declared a national emergency and said he was going to move money from the Defense Department budget to build his wall between the United States and Mexico? What do you think of that?

GOVERNOR BATT: Oh, I hate to see that because the next party will do the same in the future. It's a precedent which has been broken, and I hate to see that because we could get this green issue by the Democrats in the future. Using executive orders this way is a dangerous thing.

RG: So, you think it sets a dangerous precedent?

GOVERNOR BATT: I hate to see that kind of power put in the president to begin with.

ON RUSSIA

RG: What do you think about our relations with Russia?

GOVERNOR BATT: I have held, and still hold, that Russia is not our friend. Russia distorts our people's views without regard for the truth. I think President Trump gives too much credence in Russia's intentions. I do agree that better relations would be in everyone's interest, but we have a long way to go. I don't trust Russian bigwigs for a minute. We should be as tough as can be.

ON THE LOSS OF FAITH IN AMERICA'S INSTITUTIONS

RG: Surveys show that the American people hold almost every institution in low regard, including the president, Congress, the Supreme Court and the press. What can we do to build greater faith and trust in our institutions?

GOVERNOR BATT: I'm very discouraged. I don't know. I feel that they (politicians) are self-serving and constantly are operating to get re-elected. I believed, and still believe, in the wisdom of the people as a whole. We're still beleaguered by self-indulgent political spokespersons and bad news reporting.

RG: Do you think it would be helpful to have a stronger two-party system in Idaho?

GOVERNOR BATT: Let's just say that it would be more productive to have varying points of view on the issues. But legislators are elected proportionately to the population of the state.

ON POLITICAL GRIDLOCK IN WASHINGTON

RG: You've mentioned the gridlock in Washington a few times. You had a reputation for working well with Democrats and Republicans. Why do you think it's so hard for people to find common ground now and work together?

GOVERNOR BATT: It's probably a lot more difficult on the national scene. More partisan now. It's probably just as difficult in the Idaho legislature. Of course, the Democrats haven't had much representation in the legislature since I knocked them out when I was GOP chairman. A few more Democrats would not hurt anything. But legislators haven't found reasons to hate each other in Idaho, that I know of.

RG: Why do you think a few more Democrats in the Idaho legislature would be a good thing?

GOVERNOR BATT: Well, I'm not saying it would be, really. It would be more representative, I think, of the entire state.

RG: So, you'd like to see more bipartisanship—especially in Washington?

GOVERNOR BATT: You bet. For sure. We're killing ourselves.

ON CIVILITY IN POLITICS

RG: There seems to be less civility and respect in politics than a few years ago, or when you were active in politics. Does the current political climate concern you?

GOVERNOR BATT: The current political climate is a shameful thing. I don't have an answer for it, but it has badly injured our country worldwide and can get a lot worse. President Trump has accomplished some good things for the country, but his antagonistic style sets the tone for a lot of strife. In the meantime, it has become fashionable for politicians to hate each other. I don't like it and I'm sure Governor Andrus would be grieved by it.

Well, we're (Idaho) still better than most. It's far less civil on the national scene and I think it's a detriment to the United States to be that way.

More tolerance throughout the United States must become the norm. Violent noisy protests do little to advance one's views and are usually self-defeating. I hope people will talk more and fight less. We adults should work at getting people to discuss problems with us including politics. Young people should enter such opportunities to perfect their skills by reaching collective good results. This often involves some compromise. State your opinions, stand by your guns, but when defensible positions arise, think about signing on.

ON LISTENING TO BOTH SIDES

RG: You had one trait—and you still do—that was very uncommon among politicians back in your day and even more now in politics. And that is the ability to see both sides of an issue. Where did that ability come from?

GOVERNOR BATT: I learned a lot doing that. Just listening to one side doesn't give you a proper evaluation of it.

RG: Do you think you can make a better decision when you listen and look at both sides of an issue?

GOVERNOR BATT: Yes. Don't let the same people convince you all the time. You are better able to turn down some of the bad advice.

RG: Do you think that too many political leaders today have tunnel vision and look only at one side of an issue?

GOVERNOR BATT: Way too many in Congress. It's awful. And in Washington in general.

RG: Do you think the people read only newspapers or watch television news they agree with and that is contributing to the problem?

GOVERNOR BATT: I don't like to pick on the press, but they deserve a lot of the criticism they get for backing Democrats almost always.

RG: Of course, now we have Fox News which backs Republicans.

GOVERNOR BATT: Yeah. I watch it all the time.

ON ADMITTING WHEN YOU ARE WRONG

RG: Another trait you have had, also rare in politicians these days, is the ability to admit when you are wrong.

GOVERNOR BATT: My mother taught me that. It makes you feel better about yourself. You get it off your chest.

RG: But a lot of people don't do that, whether they're politicians or non-politicians.

GOVERNOR BATT: It is important to me. I hated admitting I was wrong. But it's better than covering it up and living with it. National politicians are terrible these days. It hardly pays to turn on the news because sometimes it makes you sick.

RG: Another trait you have is honesty.

GOVERNOR BATT: Well, a lot of people are taught like that. I'm not unique at all.

RG: It seems more important to you than some people.

GOVERNOR BATT: Mm-hmm. It benefits the person saying it.

ON HIS QUICK TEMPER

RG: Now I must ask you about a trait that isn't all that positive: you've always had a bit of a temper.

GOVERNOR BATT: Oh, yeah. I still do.

RG: Where did that come from?

GOVERNOR BATT: Oh, my dad was very quick. We put up with the tempers good in our family, all of us.

RG: It's a family trait?

GOVERNOR BATT: Yeah.

RG: But you were also good at getting over it.

GOVERNOR BATT: Oh, yeah. I'm good on that, I think.

ON THE IDAHO REPUBLICAN PARTY

RG: These days it seems like there's more than one Idaho Republican Party. Have you noticed that?

GOVERNOR BATT: Yes, I don't know how many, but there's obviously a right-wing group. The bulk of the party doesn't fit that.

RG: But that wing of the party has taken over the party infrastructure.

GOVERNOR BATT: Yeah, Kirk Sullivan was doing a fine job (as state GOP chair), working hard at it. They kicked him out because he wasn't conservative enough, I guess. [16]

RG: It seems like former congressman Raul Labrador is the leader of the right wing of the party.

GOVERNOR BATT: That's correct. He was kind of directing them. And we were so successful as Republicans. Just stupid to break us up and call each other names. It's stupid. [17]

RG: Will the factions in the party ever be repaired?

GOVERNOR BATT: Yeah, it will be someday, but I bet that other things happen before then. I think Democrats will get elected in a greater number than they are now, I'm sure.

RG: If this split continues, you think there will be more Democrats elected in the future?

GOVERNOR BATT: I think we're going to have to get over painting ourselves strictly as right-wingers. It hasn't paid to do so. We're losing a bunch of people who used to be party activists. They're just losing them to the right-wingers to doing active things in the party. And I don't think that'll last forever, surely. I don't know.

RG: Many long-time Republicans, including you, have been called RINOs—Republicans in Name Only—by other members of your party. What do you think of them labeling you a RINO?

GOVERNOR BATT: I have been a Republican all my life. I have done a lot of work for Republicans because I believe that they have the best theories towards addressing the needs of national, state and local questions for the benefit of the citizens. I've been called a RINO, and I'm not particularly offended by that. But I plead not guilty. I've done my best to save taxpayers money, and with good success. I've held state budgets down to the best practical figures. For instance, when I became governor, I finished with the least number of state employees than when I started. I believe this is unique to me.

When I chaired the Idaho Republican Party, I tried to get the party to be a big tent. A political party must include people who do not adhere to the party line.

ON IDAHO'S INFRASTRUCTURE

RG: Another issue that you cared about when you were in the legislature and then when you were chair of the Idaho Transportation Board is the state's infrastructure.

GOVERNOR BATT: Yes. I'm thinking of the road to McCall. It needs a lot of work to be safe. It's not safe at all.

RG: Do you get frustrated that we do not spend enough on infrastructure?

GOVERNOR BATT: Let's try to get some additions to it. We just raised the gas tax over six or eight years (ago). In fact, I pushed one of them through. That was the last one. I guess they got something here a while back. Just put some more in the gas tax. It's not going to kill anybody.

RG: Former governor Butch Otter used to say that by not fixing our infrastructure we are essentially deficit spending because we are leaving the investments to future generations to make.

GOVERNOR BATT: Correct. Absolutely right.

RG: Why do you think there's such a foot dragging on spending for infrastructure?

GOVERNOR BATT: People thinking they're being conservative in not spending money, but we all use the highways.

RG: Being chair of the Transportation Board was an important role you played.

GOVERNOR BATT: It was, and I enjoyed the Highway Board. I got the road paved from Greenleaf to Caldwell. It is a good road now.

RG: During his fourth term, Governor Andrus appointed you to the Idaho Transportation Board.

GOVERNOR BATT: I was a good, logical choice for a seat on the Idaho Transportation Board. I had a long interest in transportation. I knew quite a bit about it, worked hard with the board and, I believe, we did a creditable job. The board and the department still do a good job. I believe the legislature made a grievous error in borrowing federal money. We've never before received money with future contracted repayment. I hope we don't again.

ON RESTORING THE WILD SALMON

RG: The restoration of Idaho's historic salmon runs was an issue when you were governor and it still is an issue.

GOVERNOR BATT: Yeah, it's still very much an issue. Very much has its champions on both sides. [18]

RG: Even when you were governor, there was talk about removing the three dams on the lower Snake River to bring back the salmon runs. What do you think about removing those dams?

GOVERNOR BATT: Well, they're coming a lot closer to protecting the salmon than they used to be, and removing the dams would not be in our best interest. But we've got to protect the salmon.

RG: At one point, you laid out two or three issues that should be addressed before a decision is made regarding the dams. What should we be discussing?

GOVERNOR BATT: It's in the big interest of Lewiston to have a dam in there. We wouldn't have any barge traffic. It would hurt us bad, in some respects.

RG: But what if the wild salmon do go extinct?

GOVERNOR BATT: Well, we'd all regret it, some more than others. I'd consider it to be very hurtful to Idaho to have that happen.

ON HIS MENAGERIE OF PETS

RG: You have always been surrounded by pets. When you were Senate president pro tem you had a bird in your office named

Birdie. You had Sniffer the dog. Now you have a golden retriever named Sullivan or Sully. Why have you always had so many animals around you?

GOVERNOR BATT: Oh, most people do, and they're wise to do that. This dog (he points to Sully, who is resting at his feet) is the friendliest, smartest dog. Just a great dog.

RG: I remember coming into your office for an interview and your bird, Birdie, would start jabbering at me.

GOVERNOR BATT: He had about thirty good words. He could say, "Cecil is silly" every time I asked him to. (Governor Batt smiles at this)

RG: I remember him giving other people a hard time, including nosey reporters.

GOVERNOR BATT: Yeah. Right.

ON THE IMPORTANCE OF MUSIC

RG: Music seems to have played a significant role in your life. I think your first instrument was a fiddle.

GOVERNOR BATT: Yes, I had a fiddle to begin with. Well, a tonette first and then a fiddle.

RG: A tonette?

GOVERNOR BATT: Yes. They still sell them, I think. Miniature clarinet, kind of.

RG: Then you had a fiddle, and then you had your clarinet.

GOVERNOR BATT: Yes, and a saxophone, also. I played in dance bands for quite a while.

RG: You played while you attended the University of Idaho.

GOVERNOR BATT: Yeah. That was mostly tenor sax at that point. I took the clarinet. It was being played a little bit, but mostly sax.

RG: You played with some greats. Chet Atkins came and played at your inaugural.

GOVERNOR BATT: That's correct. That was a lot of fun.

RG: It must have been a thrill, playing with Chet Atkins.

GOVERNOR BATT: It was, really, and I was playing pretty good at the time, too.

RG: You played with Lionel Hampton, too.

GOVERNOR BATT: Yeah, up at the University of Idaho quite a bit.

RG: I hear you are still playing music once a month.

GOVERNOR BATT: Yeah.

RG: Where do you play?

GOVERNOR BATT: Willow Park. It's an assisted living center.

ON PRESIDENT TRUMP

RG: What do you think of President Donald Trump?

GOVERNOR BATT: Got to be careful of what I say. I voted for Trump. I'm with him on a lot of things, but he is too . . . he insults everybody too much. Insults everybody, and countries, and everything. I just don't like that.

RG: So, you disagree with his style of governing?

GOVERNOR BATT: Yeah. Well, not just style, but he ought to work with people and get it together a little bit. He's insulting all of these folks.

RG: You think he should be more collaborative and work with people?

GOVERNOR BATT: Yes.

RG: That was more your style.

GOVERNOR BATT: Thank you.

RG: Many believe that President Trump has moved the Republican Party away from traditional Republican values like supporting allies, free trade and balancing the federal budget. Do you believe President Trump has moved the party away from these values?

GOVERNOR BATT: At 93 years old, I have little comment about current national affairs. I have not been pleased with many of Trump's actions. I voted for him, but would be reluctant to do it again.

RG: Do you think President Trump should have been impeached?

GOVERNOR BATT: I do not think the case was clearly made that the president should be impeached. His re-election is approaching. I have been critical of President Trump on how he speaks of people. I think our president should embrace the historical legacy of this marvelous country.

ON CECIL ANDRUS

RG: Now I would like to ask you about a few people you knew personally in life, met or followed from a distance.

GOVERNOR BATT: Okay.

RG: I would like to start by asking you about Cecil Andrus.

GOVERNOR BATT: Andrus was elected to the Senate in 1961, I was elected to the House in 1965. We met but had no close relationship. After reapportionment, Canyon County was awarded three seats in the Senate instead of only one. I had no opposition to claim one of those seats in 1967.

I had no impression of Andrus until the next term. I then viewed him as an active leader—very firm in his opinions but full of humor—we bantered back and forth. I had a mynah bird, Birdie, which I brought to the floor, out of session. My bird knew thirty English words. I taught him to say "Cecil is silly," over and over.

Most of my discussions with Cecil were full of humor designed to deprecate the other guy. I'm sure he prayed for forgiveness.

We weren't close on a friendship basis. We didn't do anything together (socially), but he was a good man. A very good man. He was interested in different things than I was. Our main (shared) interest was the nuclear waste thing. He wanted to change some of the federal lands to make sure they were protected. And I wasn't really interested in that. I wasn't against it, but it wasn't something we shared together.

Both Cecil and I expanded our horizon to know the diversity of our state. I learned a lot from him about logging, mining and the beauty of north Idaho. He came to appreciate the skills we farmers had, but a lot of our conversation was light-hearted.

Our political philosophies did not match much. He was more prone to forming a government agency to solve problems than I was. I was more in favor of a small government, saving tax money and leaving people alone as much as possible. The politics had little to do with our friendship. We were finally thrust in together when he dumped the nuclear waste issue in my lap.

Andrus and I didn't discuss the bills much, we were mostly into humor. Once he told me that I should support kindergartens. I started public school when I was five-and-a-half years old and it seemed to serve me well. He convinced me to support it. He was right.

One thing I liked about Andrus is that he stated his positions clearly. I think he and I were similar in that we didn't have to wait for a public opinion measurement. We didn't always agree but each of us was comfortable with our own decisions.

RG: You and Governor Andrus were golfing buddies.

GOVERNOR BATT: We initially proposed a golf match and we played once a year. We were terrible golfers. He was a tall drink of water and could hit the ball a long way. Hard to say where it would land. I was much shorter in stature and strength. At first, I had the edge but as years went by, he could usually luck out and win the small purse. Andrus and I didn't often talk of politics but discussed the bad iron shots and putts the other person made. Afterward we had a cool one, reluctantly paid our paltry bets, maybe had a bite to eat. Of course, I was cranky handing money to an inferior golfer. Occasionally I would get some of his.

We never joined each other for social activities. I played my clarinet wherever anyone would let me, and he and Carol had their own activities. For the most part I saw Republicans socially and I presume he saw Democrats.

RG: But you and Governor Andrus did seem to have a unique relationship.

GOVERNOR BATT: It has become uncommon to bridge the gap between parties and to treat members as someone to argue with but reluctant to hate. There has always been some bitterness between individuals, but most people don't concentrate upon it. Most people, in politics or not, enjoy talking with and associating with others who respond with humor or keen interest. Cecil Andrus and I were only unique because of our prominence. Many others put politics in its proper place and use their best qualities to get along in this world. It was more common in the past. I hope it will be again.

ON OTHER PEOPLE HE KNEW, MET OR SERVED WITH

RG: Ronald Reagan.

GOVERNOR BATT: I liked him a lot. I really admired him. He had such a marvelous sense of humor. He could be tough when he wanted to be. He told the Russians to get the wall down, and nobody else could've done that, really.

RG: John F. Kennedy.

GOVERNOR BATT: I was inspired by Kennedy's youth and enthusiasm although I didn't vote for him. The United States should always be grateful to him for chasing Russia out of Cuba. It was a tragic event when he was assassinated, and I mourned with most others.

RG: Bill Coors.

GOVERNOR BATT: In the 1960s, hop growers did not sell directly to brewers. There were three large dealers that handled all those transactions. I had a little airplane and decided to fly over there (to Golden, Colorado) and talk to the Coors people, and see if I could sell them some hops direct. Bill Coors was so fascinated that I would fly over that he bought my hops right there.

RG: He bought the hops right on the spot?

GOVERNOR BATT: Yeah, 1,500 bales. No one else had ever

done it that I know of. So that opened up the trading mechanism and everybody does it now.

RG: Ernie Stensgar, chair of the Coeur d'Alene Tribe.

GOVERNOR BATT: Well, he was a very results-oriented person. He started talking about the things he wanted to work on together with me. We really hit it off.

RG: When you were elected governor, he asked you to create an Indian advisory committee.

GOVERNOR BATT: On the first day I took office, several Indians came in, representing various tribes. They wanted to know who from the administration would be their contact. I said, "I'm your contact." I met with them every month from then on.

RG: Governor John Evans.

GOVERNOR BATT: John Evans was a good man, and he was a good governor. I thought I could do better, and I came within one percent of beating him. But I liked John, always. He cared about the state a lot.

RG: Marilyn Shuler, the long-time executive director of the Idaho Human Rights Commission.

GOVERNOR BATT: I always admired her. Of course, she was a big Democrat, but she was very brave. She didn't mind saying what she thought on anything. And we got along really well.

RG: Gene Harris, world-renowned jazz pianist who lived in Boise.

GOVERNOR BATT: He was a marvelous guy . . . I used to go down there (to the Idanha Hotel) every month . . . I sat in on some of the tunes, jazz, mainly. We had a great time, and I think entertained a lot of people.

RG: Governor Butch Otter.

GOVERNOR BATT: Butch is a good man. He put up with me good when he was lieutenant governor under me and assisted me in any way I asked.

RG: Governor Dirk Kempthorne.

GOVERNOR BATT: Dirk was a good public servant. The state ran smoothly under his leadership.

RG: He also managed your first campaign for governor in 1982.

GOVERNOR BATT: Yeah. Well, he was a good man for that job. We almost won it.

RG: Governor Brad Little.

GOVERNOR BATT: I've known Brad for a long time, and he's a good man. I think he can be a great governor.

RG: He considers you a mentor.

GOVERNOR BATT: Well, I'm flattered about that. Of course, I knew his father. He was a senator. He was one of the standard old-timers.

RG: Senator Jim Risch.

GOVERNOR BATT: I have supported his career in the past and am supporting it today.

I served with Senator Risch in most of his political career. Senator Risch does meet my expectations as a U.S. senator. He is smart and knows how to get things done. He exerts the power of attracting allies for worthwhile legislative projects.

Senator Risch keeps track of his service. On occasion he will correct his views and he is not afraid to admit when he makes a mistake.

RG: George H. W. Bush.

GOVERNOR BATT: Yeah, I got to meet him. Talked with him a little bit. I greatly admired him. I think he had tremendous goodwill toward other people, and I think he did a great job as president.

RG: Bill Hall, the former editorial page editor of The Lewiston Morning Tribune.

GOVERNOR BATT: Oh, yeah. (He smiles at the mention of Bill Hall.) I got along with Bill fine. We talked about everything, on opposite sides quite a bit. He was a good man.

RG: He carried your column on the Tribune's editorial page.

GOVERNOR BATT: Oh, yes. Always. We got along good.

RG: Do you remember sparring with him?

GOVERNOR BATT: We didn't mind disagreeing in public. It's alright.

ON RECEIVING THE IDAHO CIVILIAN MEDAL

RG: Earlier this year you received the Idaho Medal of Achievement Award—the highest honor any Idahoan can receive.

GOVERNOR BATT: I was very pleased with that.

RG: Your medal is heavy—it's made with silver.

GOVERNOR BATT: I'm going to take it to a pawnshop (he laughs).

RG: Governor Otter might not be too happy if you do that.

GOVERNOR BATT: You know what? It's kind of weird that they'd (give it to) anybody that was in politics. I bet they'll wait a long time before they put another politician in there.

RG: Why do you think that?

GOVERNOR BATT: There's too many outstanding people that are outstanding in their own right without getting in politics.

RG: Were you surprised to receive it?

GOVERNOR BATT: Oh, very much.

RG: How did they notify you that you had received it?

GOVERNOR BATT: Well, Eva Gay told me. [19]

EVA GAY: Well, I had to tell him in order to get him to go to the ceremony and receive it.

GOVERNOR BATT: They were going to make it a surprise.

EVA GAY: We (Eva Gay and Francee, Governor Batt's wife) thought about every way to try to make it a surprise . . . You see, he already had to be at the statehouse on Friday for the inauguration of Governor Little, and Saturday for the inaugural ball and the dinner. They were going to give him the medal on Thursday. Well, he was already concerned about having to be gone from home so much.

GOVERNOR BATT: I got mad.

EVA GAY: We decided that he wouldn't go to the ceremony if we didn't tell him that he was going to receive the medal.

A FEW FINAL WORDS

RG: Idahoans want to know how Idaho's longest-living governor is doing at age ninety-three.

GOVERNOR BATT: My first wife, Jacque, and I were married in 1948. She expired sixty-six years later after a series of debilitating illnesses. We have three children, numerous grandkids and other relatives. I was fortunate to win Francee Reilly's hand later. We've now been married four years. She was a sister of Terry Reilly. She is a wonderful mate for me. [20]

RG: The last question: What did you think of this conversation?

GOVERNOR BATT: I kind of enjoyed it.

Top, from left: Jim, Emma, Ruth, John. Bottom, from left: John (father), Phil, Elizabeth (mother).

Top, from left: Phil, Jim, John. Bottom, from left: Ruth, John (father), Elizabeth (mother), Emma.

Wilder High School photo.

A Canyon County farmer with his bounty of very, very big onions.

Photo courtesy of the Idaho State Archives.

Batt campaigning for governor in 1982 with then-Vice President George H.W. Bush. *Photo courtesy of the Idaho State Archives.*

Governor Batt and First Lady Jacque Batt arriving at the Inaugural Ball in 1995. *Photo courtesy of the Idaho State Archives.*

With his children (left to right) Rebecca, Bill and Leslie.

ESSAYS

C.L "BUTCH" OTTER Otter brings more than 40 years of state, national and global public policy and business experience to his Of Counsel role with Sullivan & Reberger. Butch is a living legend in Idaho politics – winning election to two terms in the Idaho House of Representatives, four terms as Lieutenant Governor, and three terms representing western and northern Idaho in Congress, then capping a distinguished public service career with three terms as Governor. His years as Idaho's chief executive saw him lead the state through the Great Recession without raising taxes or eliminating vital government services. Butch's background as an international agribusiness executive helped him build bipartisan coalitions behind unprecedented improvements to Idaho's public schools. He championed historic tax relief and brought competing interests together on hard-won agreements to preserve and protect Idaho's precious water resources. Butch also was instrumental in creation of two community colleges and Idaho's first medical school during his tenure, and he was the driving force behind Idaho's landmark state-based health insurance exchange. That commitment to long-term thinking enables him to provide unique context and perspective to any enterprise.

Outgoing Gov. Butch Otter waves to the crowd during the State of Idaho Forty-Eighth Inauguration ceremonies, Friday, Jan. 4, 2019. Photo courtesy of Brian Myrick/Idaho Press.

Former Governor C.L. "Butch" Otter

The Phil Batt I know is the same one everyone knows. No secret agendas, no different treatment of people depending on who they are, rarely a reversal of a position. In sum, what you see is the complete Phil Batt. And what you see is what you get.

Phil and I were, for a time, competitors in the onion-packing business—he with his Allendale (Wilder, Idaho) operation; me with the Simplot sheds in Ontario and Nyssa, Oregon. These operations, from time to time, brought us together, in an effort to address problems or opportunities that our respective operations shared. We worked on solutions—planting, harvesting and packing shipping problems—with the rest of the area packing sheds.

Phil's leadership improved our industry's operations and reputation. The biggest victory was getting Japan as a buyer of the Gentle Giant (yellow sweet Spanish onions). That is a market still growing in volume today.

My eventual entrance into politics came as a result of a suggestion by Phil Batt when he was Senate majority leader.

It was 1972 and the legislative session had ended by early spring. Senator Batt was offering a legislative "wrap-up" report to the Caldwell Chamber of Commerce at a noon luncheon. During his report, Senator Batt noted that Representatives Clyde Keithly and Jerry Jenkins, who represented legislative District Twelve (half of Canyon County) in the House, had both announced their retirement. With me sitting in the audience and to my surprise, Phil suggested that C.L. "Butch" Otter should consider running for one of those vacant seats. Hence, his comments launched my political career.

Two terms (four years) in the Idaho House of Representatives; four terms (fourteen years) as lieutenant governor; three terms (six years) in the U.S. House of Representatives; and three terms (twelve years) as governor. Thirty-six years in office with forty-nine opponents, all because of a Phil Batt suggestion.

Aside from being one of my primary mentors, Phil also served as my honorary chairman in several of my campaigns, and his daughter, Rebecca, managed my first successful statewide campaign for lieutenant governor.

From January 1995 until January 1999, I was Governor Batt's lieutenant governor. During that four years, he felt the lieutenant governor could, and should, be treated and educated as to the operations of the executive branch of government.

Always the optimist, Governor Batt gave me duties that I doubt any previous lieutenant governor had been trusted with. I believe his own term as lieutenant governor (1979-1983) convinced him that the position could be of value to the state and should be put to practical use. So, he did.

Always the humorist, Phil one time told me, "Butch, you are the most useful lieutenant governor any governor could hope for. I can use you as both a good example, or a bad example." Governor Batt was given to make that affectionate statement because I had made several bad decisions of a personal nature that became widely publicized. His intent, I believe, was to suggest that all was understood and forgiven.

So, Phil has sure been an example to me in my business, public and personal life: "They need love the most when they appear to deserve it the least."

Phil has been a great leader for the state of Idaho. I only regret that he was not born twins.

Inscription on the Idaho Medal of Honor

In his last official act as governor, Governor Butch Otter awards former Governor Phil Batt the Idaho Medal of Achievement, the highest civilian honor the State of Idaho bestows. Governor-elect Brad Little looks on. *Photo courtesy of Brian Myrick/Idaho Press.*

DIRK KEMPTHORNE served as the 30th Governor of Idaho from 1999-2006. He resigned from the governorship in 2006 to become the 49th U.S. Secretary of Interior under President George W. Bush. Kempthorne was elected mayor of Boise at the age of 34 in 1986 and served until 1993. He served one term in the U.S. Senate from 1993 to 1999 when he returned to Idaho to serve as Governor.

Photo courtesy of Dirk Kempthorne.

Former Governor Dirk Kempthorne

My first experience with Phil Batt, ironically, was not so much in his role as a public servant, but as a musician. It was a great pleasure to go to the Idanha Hotel, in downtown Boise, and listen to him play his clarinet with the great jazz artist, Gene Harris. I remember the beautiful rapport and friendship those two had. The music these musicians made together, with others who would sit in, was wonderful. It was such a positive and fun atmosphere. It is a wonderful memory for me. And not just the music, but the look of joy on each of their faces, and the banter they would exchange between songs. You could tell they were dear friends who admired one another greatly.

I remember one night a few years after those first encounters, I had just flown back to the Boise airport and my wife, Patricia, was there to meet me. As we headed through the lobby, we saw Idaho's lieutenant governor, Phil Batt. We went over and said hello, and he was very friendly and cordial. I asked what brought him to the airport, and he said he was flying that night to eastern Idaho. I was surprised by the fact that he was all alone.

As Patricia and I started to head to the car, I remember the strong feeling I had that our lieutenant governor surely should not be alone, so we turned and went back, asking if he'd like us to wait with him for his flight. He politely declined and said he was just fine, and for us to head on home. It wasn't until years later, when I was in the role as a public servant, that I realized how nice it was at times to have some private time.

In 1982, when Phil decided to run for governor of Idaho, he began putting together a campaign organization. My good friend Mark Dunn was very close to Phil, and he suggested to Phil that I would be a good campaign manager. I had a meeting with Phil in his office and he offered me the job. I remember two feelings as I left his office. One, I was proud to be part of serving a man I admired and believed in; and two, that there would be enormous and important work ahead if this was going to be done right.

Working with Phil on a daily basis during the campaign, I shared in a variety of experiences with this man and his family. They are a very close family and their love for one another was very apparent. You could see they were absolutely devoted to him and to the goal of his becoming governor.

One time, when we took a break from campaigning, he said he'd like to take me fishing to his favorite fishing hole at Sinker Creek. The two of us set out early one morning hiking up into the Owyhee Mountains with our fishing poles and his supply of Hi-Ho crackers and cheese for our lunch. We hiked over some rugged spots, but we eventually got to this beautiful setting of crystal-clear water rushing over the rocks. And sure enough, we caught a number of small and beautiful rainbow trout. We headed back to Phil's home, and Jacque had cooked up a beautiful dinner of fried chicken. It was a very nice day for me with the candidate and his family around their kitchen table.

On another occasion, Phil invited me to come back out to Canyon County to join him and one of his best friends, Frankie Garrett, for a threesome of golf. When I got there, I experienced first-hand the frugality of Phil Batt. He told me that he was paying the golf fees for Frankie and himself but that I had to pay my own. He also told me he and Frankie were renting a golf cart, but I'd have to walk.

I kind of gulped a little, hoping I had enough cash, because at thirty years old, with two little kids at home, Patricia and I didn't have a lot of financial freedom. Oh well . . . I will say that Frankie was a delight to meet and be with. He and Phil were pals. On one hole there was an abundance of starlings squawking loudly on the ground by the T-box. Frankie simply tossed one of his clubs toward the birds to get them to leave. It was a gentle toss, but it actually connected with one of the birds who was momentarily stunned by the club. Phil began chortling that Frankie had finally gotten a birdie on this golf course. When the game was over Phil asked me if I wanted to have a drink and something to eat with the two of them. I knew I didn't have another dime in my pocket, so I made up some excuse that I had to get going.

Phil won the primary. It was a good night for celebration . . . for most. Phil took me aside that night and told me he wasn't happy with the campaign organization during the primary. His rationale was that he felt he had been well-enough known and thought of around the state that he didn't need all that campaign stuff to win the primary. He said he was thinking of making changes. Boom. So much for the celebration. Not a high point for me. While it was very disappointing to hear his reaction, I respectfully and politely pointed out that all of that campaign stuff that we had put together, such as the organization in every county, and the volunteers and phone banks throughout the state, was not merely for the primary, it was for the main event, a campaign against a very tough, popular opponent, the incumbent governor of Idaho, John Evans. Our organization was now primed and ready to cover every community in the state.

The next morning, I got a call from Phil Batt saying, "Let's get this thing going." There was never again a mention or reference to the conversation we had had the night before.

It was a tough campaign. I remember right after the primary a meeting Phil had in his office with a few of us, including one of the best political strategists in Idaho, Phil Reberger. This meeting had the sole purpose to hear what former governor Bob Smylie felt was necessary to win. His message to Phil was tough with incredibly blunt and colorful words. We all knew we had a big challenge ahead.

I can speak from experience when I say that I know that campaigns can be grinding on a candidate. Even with all of the wonderful people that support you, the volunteers that work long hours tirelessly for your victory, the family members that love you and give you encouragement, a campaign can be taxing. Some people, like Idaho's former U.S. senator Steve Symms, love campaigning, but that wasn't always the case with Phil Batt.

After a long weekend of Phil campaigning across the state, I would inevitably get a call first thing Monday morning from Hazel Keefer, Phil's wonderful secretary. She'd say, "You need to get over here right away, Phil wants to talk to you." And each time I would ask, "How is his mood?" she would inevitably say, "Oh, my, you just need to get over here." So, I'd head to Phil's office, with notepad in hand. And then Phil, in no uncertain terms, told me about every annoyance, frustration, snafu, that he had experienced the past few days, and when was I going to fix it? They were not pleasant conversations, but I learned to develop a poker face, take good notes, and then fix whatever needed fixing or realigning. I think it actually was great training ground when years later I would be in my own campaigns and had that same poker face during some eight statewide debates I had.

But those of us who know and love Phil Batt know that his quick temper will give way to his better angel. By afternoon he'd often feel remorse from some of the things he had said, and you were on sound footing again. Monday mornings were hell, Monday afternoons were much better, and most often things would go well the rest of the week . . . until the next Monday morning, when I would get the call from Hazel.

Now it wasn't always pure stress and lack of fun. I will always remember one time being asked to come out to his farm in Wilder for a meeting. When I arrived, I saw the creativity of his children, Rebecca, Bill, and Leslie. There, in the driveway, was Phil's bright green Ford Fiesta with bats painted all over it and the words, "Batt for Governor!" Unbeknownst to me was the fact that the entire family, including Phil, was hiding out of sight to watch and see what my reaction was to this iconic car. I think they worried that I wouldn't think it was in keeping with the dignity of the office, but my reaction was, let's use every positive element we can to capture people's attention. And this car sure did that! The Batt-mobile put on thousands of miles and was in a myriad of parades.

I would travel with the candidate whenever I could. One particular afternoon, Phil had just finished an event in Sun Valley, and he and I had to drive to eastern Idaho. During one stretch of the trip across the desert, he wanted to try on me his entire repertoire of humorous stories. Phil loves humor. So, while I drove the now famous Batt-mobile, I was treated, for well over an hour, to Phil Batt's brand of humor. Some were absolute gems . . . others were bombs.

We would both be laughing at the good ones, but when I would groan at some of the others, he would ask me to rank them. We devised an audience reaction meter that cleverly was my arm. A true gem received the arm bent at the elbow ninety degrees so that the hand was pointing up to the sky. A less-than-stellar joke was simply the arm straight out—in other words, a flatline—the joke was dead. He'd argue over some of my rulings, but I reminded him that I had charge of the audience meter. He would then remind me that he was the candidate. It's funny how that admonition improved the reaction to his jokes.

I will let others give the details and blow-by-blow of the general election. It was an extremely close election. Probably no one knows that around ten p.m. on election night, when it looked like Phil Batt was going to be elected, he pulled me aside to say how the state was so divided over labor issues, and that later that week, as the governor-elect, he wanted me to reach out to the union leadership, to set up a meeting so he could talk to them. Phil knows you can disagree without being disagreeable.

His first reaction was not to bask in the glory of what, at that moment, appeared to be a victory, but to already be thinking about how he would govern, which included reaching out to groups not in your camp. Later that night, the perceived victory evaporated, and so did the opportunity to show what kind of governor Phil Batt would be. But ultimately, history would create a chapter devoted to the legacy of Governor Phil Batt.

I would also like to say that although I was the campaign manager that set out to unseat Governor John Evans, he and Lola were always gracious to me and to my family. And when I became governor, I had fine conversations with John. We became friends. This is the essence of Idaho politics. We can still treat one another with respect.

And it is here that I must point out that, following the campaign, Phil Batt the miser continued to pay me a salary after the campaign, until I could get back on my feet with another job. Patricia and I are so grateful for that generosity . . . and humanity.

When Phil Batt did become our governor, I admired how he governed. I admired how he never shirked a responsibility of leadership. There are any number of decisions a governor must make, and Phil made them with sincerity and honor and dignity.

He dealt with tough issues, such as a human life, when he appointed a committee of one—himself—to review the case of a convicted murderer who faced the death penalty, and to have that sentence commuted by Governor Batt. I remember the time when, as a U.S. senator, I stood next to Governor Batt on the banks of the dangerously swollen Clearwater River in Orofino. Governor Batt, while consoling the family, had to give the order to the National Guard to knock down that family's house because as the river rose, it would ultimately float the house off of its foundation and send the entire structure into the Orofino bridge, causing terrible consequences, such as the loss of the bridge itself. He knew how to make very tough decisions. He reined in the growth of government.

So many of us were impressed with his leadership and his transparent style that a great disappointment arose when he indicated he would not run for a second term. I went to him to strongly—in fact, emphatically—encouraging him to continue his leadership for a second term. I brought with me a wonderful book, a biography of George Washington, and I wrote an entire inscription on the inside page of the book, pointing out how Washington needed a second term to firmly put in place all that he had started. I said, "This is the same for you, my friend, to finish what you have so successfully started."

His ultimate decision to not seek a second term caused me to wrestle with an extremely difficult decision, whether to leave the U.S. Senate and run for governor of Idaho. I know it was important for Phil that our party retain the office of governor. This was one of the toughest decisions I ever had to face.

A very short time before the day that I had scheduled for a news conference to announce my decision, I was at our Boise condo weighing the issue. Early that morning there was a knock on the door. I wasn't expecting anyone and no one else was home but me. I opened the door and standing there was Governor Batt. It was a total surprise. I welcomed him inside. He said he wanted to talk about the campaign and who would replace him on the Republican ticket. I said we had outstanding candidates that could become our next governor. He said he didn't disagree. We were blessed with fine individuals . . . and their time would come. He repeated, their time would come.

In that he was prophetic. Wonderful people like Jim Risch and Butch Otter would become great governors of Idaho. And we're now blessed to have another dear friend and University of Idaho schoolmate of mine, Brad Little, as our outstanding governor. And on the national level, two greatly-admired and effective leaders in Congress, Senator Mike Crapo and Congressman Mike Simpson. That team is now enhanced with Russ Fulcher. And now with Jim Risch in the U.S. Senate, a great Idaho team remains in place—all dear friends of mine, and ironically, I had the great pleasure of appointing both Brad and Russ to the Idaho Senate during my term as governor.

But that morning, Phil told me that at this time, I needed to come home and be a candidate for governor. I just looked at him. And he said it again, "It is time." We discussed the particulars for a short time and then he left. I made the decision to come home and be a candidate for governor and leave the Senate. After a tough race, we won.

I was extremely grateful for the confidence the people of Idaho put in me by electing me governor. That night, there was a victory speech, a celebration with all the great volunteers, then some cherished private time at home with my loving family, and a prayer I offered to God for guidance.

The next day I wanted to see the man who I had always admired, whose place I would take, and whose success I would strive to continue. But I suppose I should have been more sensitive to the bittersweet moment it was for Governor Batt. Here was a man who knew he would have been reelected, who had dedicated so much of his life to public service, and was at the pinnacle of one of the great political positions, the governor of a sovereign state, the great state of Idaho.

As the governor-elect, I had immediate new demands: Set up a transition, determine who to ask to serve our state in leadership positions, prepare a multi-million-dollar budget, and a myriad of other decisions to make in a relatively short time frame. In other words, get ready to govern. And I sought insight from the man I had asked to stay in this office, a man I had always admired.

Ironically, it may have been a time similar to the meeting in the Boise airport years ago, when what he needed right then was a little time alone, to reflect on all he had accomplished and the good memories he had to savor. The two different needs, I believe, put a strain on our relationship. Perhaps ironically, but also perhaps, understandably.

Now, we're back to having good conversations and sharing good laughs. Patricia and I are so happy for this current phase of true happiness that Phil is enjoying with Francee. I am so happy for my friend. I sent them a letter upon their marriage offering my heartfelt congratulations. Because they probably did not need material things, I said I had a different kind of gift for them.

My position at the time caused me to travel internationally. So, as time permitted, and still to this day, I like to go to local places of faith, such as the iconic and beautiful Cathedral of Notre Dame in Paris. I told Phil and Francee that just as I had already done for them in Notre Dame, I would light a candle for them in places of worship I would visit, as a prayer, for their continued happiness, health, and love.

Phil Batt deserves the thanks of all of us in Idaho. And I will continue to light a candle for my friend.

MARC JOHNSON has been a broadcast journalist and the chief of staff to former Idaho governor Cecil Andrus. He was also a communications and crisis management consultant with the Gallatin Group. He is the author of *Political Hell-Raiser: The Life and Times of Senator Burton K. Wheeler of Montana. Tuesday Night Massacre* is his book on the 1980 election in which the Republican Party defeated enough sitting senators, including Senator Frank Church of Idaho, to take control of the U.S. Senate for the first time in a generation.
Photo courtesy of Marc Johnson.

Marc Johnson

My first memory of Phil Batt is really a memory of his mynah bird, Woodstock. It must have been around 1978 and I was a very green reporter trying to make sense of the Idaho legislature when the Republican senator, then-president pro tem of the Senate, invited a few of us into his office to see and hear his talking bird.

How can you not like a politician with a talking pet bird?

Woodstock, or as Batt called him, "Birdie," would often answer questions by saying, "Cecil is like that," or "Cecil is silly," a reference to my old boss and Batt's old friend, Governor Cecil Andrus.

Batt once quoted legendary Idaho Statesman reporter John Corlett as saying "Birdie" knew thirty-five or forty sentences, "more than the average state senator."

When Woodstock died in 1980—Phil had become lieutenant governor—Batt said the bird expired after watching Democratic governor John Evans' State of the State speech. Either Evans' "pear shaped tones excited my feathery friend to an unbearable degree" or perhaps Woodstock had seen Batt sitting in behind Evans and, Batt said, concluded "I was being held captive."

As I said, how can you not like this guy?

It can also be safely admitted all these years later that Phil, the buttoned-down, reserved politician, enjoyed a drink from time to time, even tippling inside the supposedly dry capitol building. In those days, the press center was deep in the basement of the statehouse and more than a few times during the legislative session Batt would make his way down to the press caverns to have a nip of whatever libation Jim Fisher, the political reporter for the Lewiston Tribune, had in his bottom desk drawer.

Everything was off the record in these sessions, of course, and Batt was always at his typically candid and often very funny best. He enjoyed a bawdy story, particularly if it was at the expense of a stuffed shirt in the legislature. It was a different era, when reporters benefited from the unfiltered insights of an insider and a politician could build trust and respect among the scribblers. They were different days, and yes, better days.

I'm sure Batt got his share of bad press and he would, as all politicians do, complain about it, but when Phil wrote his sort of memoir twenty years ago, he actually thanked what he called the "newsies," saying, "I always did love ya', even though it sometimes wasn't evident."

I developed an even fuller picture of the man as I covered Batt's unsuccessful 1982 gubernatorial race against John Evans, a contest that might well have turned on the release of a stupid and sleazy comic book that depicted Evans as a stooge of organized labor. The Associated Press wondered whether the comic book distorting Evans' record would "backfire and hurt Batt's campaign." It likely did.

Batt disavowed the hit piece that was financed by an independent group that was allegedly trying to help his campaign, but Republican Party leaders never really repudiated the negative tactics and Phil lost by 4,200 votes. I think the loss stung him bitterly—it would have stung anyone—and when asked if he might run again, Batt said, "I'll just say it's unlikely." That was one of his bad predictions.

Phil Batt's second act wasn't long coming, and I got to know him better thanks to the rare political and personal friendship he enjoyed with my political mentor, Cece Andrus. In many respects, Andrus and Batt were polar opposites: the diminutive, clarinet-playing onion farmer from Wilder and the strapping, elk-hunting lumberjack from Orofino. Yet, in so many other ways, they were very much alike.

Both lived by the old code that your word is your bond. Andrus couldn't pay a higher compliment than to say that a political friend or foe was "a man of his word." He always said that about Phil.

Both were as honest as the day is long. Both loved a good joke and could, unlike so many in public life, poke fun at themselves. Both could be tough partisans, but each was also a pragmatist, knowing when and how to cut a deal even if it meant settling for less than they hoped for. And both harbored a healthy respect for the office they each held and the responsibilities they exercised as governors.

At a time when so many question the importance of government or express disdain for those who work in public service, Batt and Andrus maintained what is now perhaps an old-fashioned attitude that government can and should do good and important things. They approached governing as a privilege and a duty, and an honorable one at that.

When Andrus became governor in 1987—his second life, he called it—he inherited a major mess at the state Department of Health and Welfare. A big computer project called EPICS was supposed to help process public assistance claims, but the effort was in disarray, months behind schedule and millions of dollars over budget. The state was facing federal sanctions if it wasn't corrected promptly, and even more importantly, thousands of Idahoans were being denied the help they were entitled to and needed. I was Andrus's press secretary and knew, as the governor certainly did, that we needed good advice, time to clean up the mess, and the type of credibility that didn't automatically descend on a new administration.

I remember Andrus walking into my office one morning to ask me to prepare a statement to the effect that his Republican pal, Senator Phil Batt, had agreed to investigate the computer boondoggle and make recommendations about a fix. Or to put the situation in raw political terms: a Democratic governor was putting a Republican politician in charge of helping correct a problem that had developed on the watch of the Democratic governor that same Republican had lost to four years earlier.

It's entirely possible that my facial expression betrayed my surprise at such a decision. Andrus simply said, "I trust Phil." He also knew, of course, that his own response to the computer problem would require spending more money and that Batt, given full authority to probe and prod, would not only detail the problems, but have the credibility to gain support for a costly fix.

A month later Phil presented his report—publicly—and Andrus accepted it in every detail and said what they both believed: they were committed "to properly serving those citizens who need and deserve benefits."

In the broad sweep of Idaho political history this is a minor story, mostly long forgotten, but it does illustrate the power of trust and the benefits of bipartisanship. I have thought about these details a lot in the intervening years, and realize now that Andrus had no real sense of what Batt would discover or what he would insist on saying about it, but it was enough that he "trusted Phil."

A less bipartisan tone was struck and the old friendship strained in 1990, when Andrus sought and won the last of his four terms. The Democratic governor was riding high, enjoying widespread approval. The Idaho economy was humming and educational appropriations were enjoying significant improvements. Republicans, meanwhile, were offering only a motley collection of second-rate challengers to the governor. Phil momentarily upset the era of good feelings in a way that, at least at the time, I considered unfair and highly partisan. In retrospect, Batt made Andrus an even better governor in his final term.

Republicans were pressing Phil to run against Andrus in 1990 and when, after some deliberation, he declined the challenge, he took the opportunity to hit Andrus right on top of his bald head. Batt called his long-time friend "arrogant" and too partisan, and said he had lost touch with the people who elected him. Andrus's "two decades of political success have seriously impaired his ability to rule impartially," Batt said in statement that this time really hit Andrus hard.

Both men could have a hair trigger temper, and Andrus initially fumed at the criticism, but he was, also like Phil, among the most self-aware people I've ever encountered. Andrus reflected deeply on the stinging rebuke and after his anger subsided, he said, "When Phil Batt offers criticism, I listen."

All these years later I wonder if Phil knew, even as Andrus was headed toward a landslide re-election, that he needed to go out and work to earn a fourth term and that if he did so, his last go-round would be the better for it.

In the wake of Phil's broadside, and with Andrus's full blessing—he became determined that his last campaign would be about getting in front of as many Idahoans as humanly possible—we devised an extensive "retail political" campaign schedule and a totally positive television effort. Andrus was determined to recapture the "happy warrior" image that had for so long served him so well and that Batt was saying had slipped away.

We went to every county fair and rodeo we could schedule, rode in every parade, worked shift changes at the Simplot gate in Pocatello and the Potlatch mill in Lewiston, and mounted a 100-city bus tour to coincide with the centennial of Idaho statehood.

At one stop, in the tiny Magic Valley burg of Eden, I parked the motorhome Andrus and I were driving around the state in front of a dodgy-looking tavern in the late afternoon. The governor bounded out of the vehicle with a fistful of campaign brochures saying he wouldn't be a minute. When he returned, Andrus said there were seven guys in the bar. "I got four of them," he said smiling, "and we'll consider the other three undecideds."

Andrus won that last election with nearly seventy percent of the vote, and I've always felt that Phil Batt and his timely critique helped put the fire back in his belly.

Much has been written and said about the Batt-Andrus collaboration to hold the Department of Energy to account for its past environmental practices at the Idaho National Laboratory, and it is true that as governor, Batt created a landmark agreement with the federal government and did so with Andrus's full cooperation and support. They privately debated and occasionally disagreed about the details, but when they came to agreement, they presented a dramatically effective bipartisan front on a critical issue.

It is not an editorial opinion, but merely a fact that Idaho will live to rue the day Batt's agreement is eroded further. The two men were visionaries on a mission to protect the state and her people. They deserve to continue to be listened to.

In the post-gubernatorial years, they both played a lot of golf together and regularly exchanged political gossip. I was fortunate to be in a few foursomes with the two where the banter was often hilarious, the jokes often not fit for family ears, and the golf mediocre but nevertheless played with the competitive intensity of the final hole at the Masters.

On one occasion at Boise's Hillcrest Country Club, Phil was on the tee addressing the ball when Andrus casually asked about a rumor floating around about a certain prominent politician. Batt got to laughing, had trouble with his tee shot and accused Andrus of purposely trying to damage his score. There may have been a modest wager hanging in the balance.

I treasure the memory of Cece Andrus sauntering into my office to say that he'd just gotten off the phone with the man he called "the little giant" and had some gossip to share. Just as often I would ask what Phil was thinking about such and such and Andrus would say, "Well, that's between Phil and me."

They trusted each other, and that is the glue of politics as well as at the heart of a long, long friendship. Needless to say, I'm delighted my long-time pal Rod Gramer has pulled together this project on Governor Batt and that he asked me to offer a few reflections. I'll end with this.

Phil Batt has left his mark on so much—nuclear waste policy and human rights among many things—and he deserves a special rank in Idaho history for that, but also for being an honorable guy working hard to make politics an honorable calling. Not a bad legacy, that.

LINDY HIGH began her career as a reporter for United Press International. After working for UPI, she worked in press relations at the University of Idaho, the State Board of Education, and the Idaho Department of Health and Welfare. In 1987 she became public information officer for Jerry Evans, the Republican state school superintendent. In 1995, High joined the staff of Governor Phil Batt where she served as a senior staff assistant for his entire four-year term. After Batt decided not to run for a second term, High joined the staff of State School Superintendent Marilyn Howard, a Democrat, where she worked for the next eight years. From 1986 to 1994 High wrote a regular column for the *Idaho Statesman's* editorial page. She is retired and lives in Boise.

Photo courtesy of Lindy High.

Lindy High

I joined Governor Batt's staff a week after his 1995 inauguration. It was a hectic time: the legislature convened that day, everyone was still learning assignments, the mail was piling up, and the phones never stopped ringing. Fun fact: no one writes or calls the governor's office if things are going well.

I had known Phil Batt for many years, dating back to when I was a reporter for United Press International and he was a member of the Idaho state Senate. He was a good guy to know—witty, occasionally irreverent, smart and thoughtful, sometimes thin-skinned, open to questions about process or plans, and nice to reporters—something that wasn't always true for legislators. Years later, when I worked at the Department of Health and Welfare, then-governor Cecil Andrus asked Batt to head up a committee to examine and fix problems with DHW's new computer system. Batt was not exactly computer literate, then or later, but he had the ability to listen carefully, ask good questions, and move solutions forward.

Late in 1994, as Batt prepared for his new role as governor and began assembling his staff, he called me and invited me over to his temporary office for an interview. It was the fastest interview in history. Batt doesn't like to waste time. I think the job he offered was "policy advisor," and my assigned areas would be education, health, welfare, human rights, and a few odds and ends. I left about fifteen minutes later, slightly stunned and excited about joining the new office.

Phil Batt is a man of contradictions: good-humored but with a quick temper; frugal with public money but generous with his own; critical when things aren't moving along as he'd hoped but patient and understanding when staff members were dealing with personal problems. He was impatient with any waste of time unless the time was spent with the children who visited his office. And when young musicians gathered for their band concerts in the statehouse rotunda, Batt would often grab his clarinet and sit in with them for a while.

He was also a man who respected the office of governor—and expected others to respect it as well—but who remained humble about himself. He often ate lunch at Yen Ching, a downtown Chinese restaurant, and I once asked him why he went there so frequently. Well, he said, he liked the food, the service was good, and he could always get a table. *You're the governor*, I thought to myself. *You could probably get a table anywhere.*

Not long after Batt took office, a columnist for the *Boise Weekly* wrote a piece critical of the new staff. The writer said things were so bad that the new governor had been seen lugging an armful of green folders up the statehouse steps, meaning the state's chief executive was spending his time going through the day's accumulation of incoming mail. Surely, the writer suggested, a governor had better things to do.

The new chief of staff, Jeff Malmen, called us together to make sure we had all read the column. (I didn't think it applied to me. The columnist described Batt's new staff as being full of "young . . . zealots" and I was neither young nor a zealot.) Truth is, we were all frazzled by pretty much everything: how to work with state agencies, how to work with one another, how to work the phone system, how to handle the mail, and on and on. Batt saw what was happening and closed the office early one Friday afternoon—another thing the columnist complained about—just so we could catch up.

About the mail: the columnist's complaint notwithstanding, Batt continued through his term to browse the incoming mail every day. It was a great way for him to find out what people throughout the state were thinking, what they wanted or needed, what was going wrong, what was going right, and what issues they cared most about. Thus, Batt was the first reader of the nasty anonymous letter about nuclear waste storage in eastern Idaho, a letter that used the f-word in pretty much every sentence. Still, the writer apparently forgot that he wanted to remain anonymous, because he added his name and return address on the outside envelope. Nuclear waste storage was not one of my areas, so I never saw Batt's response to the angry writer.

The governor's practice of perusing all incoming mail was actually helpful to staff. We could tell callers that, yes, if they wrote to the governor, the governor would be the first to read the letter. And if the letter was a complaint about staff, well, again, the governor would be the first to find out.

Often Batt would write notes in the margins to tell staff members what he wanted done with the information or what he wanted the response to be. At first, he wrote "See me" when he wanted to see the staff member in person. But writing "See me" takes time—and he hated wasting time—so soon he shortened it to "SIMI." If you got three or four SIMIs in a day, you knew you had your work cut out for you.

It's a good thing "SIMI" was hard to mess up because Batt had, and probably still has, one flaw: his handwriting. He should have been a doctor because he would have had a head start on writing those unintelligible prescriptions. Once he handed me a yellow legal pad on which he'd written something he wanted me to see. I began to read. But I was reading slowly—really, the handwriting was hard to decipher—and eventually he snatched the pad out of my hands and began to briskly read out loud until . . . until . . . until he leaned down, pointed to a scribble, and asked me if I knew what that word was. I laughed so hard I almost fell out of my chair.

Batt also imposed a strict, thirty-day deadline for responding to letters. He thought everyone who took the time to write to the Office of the Governor deserved a timely and appropriate answer. The staff member who opened and distributed the mail kept records on when a letter came in and when its response went out. Anyone missing a deadline had better have a good excuse, because an overdue response meant a new SIMI to explain.

The governor's office was a congenial place to work. Batt didn't like competition among his staff members; he wanted us to work collaboratively with one another. His mantra was, "Remember, you are the servant of the people and not their master," and he said it so often we probably began repeating it in our sleep. Once I was late getting to the car when Batt and I were going to some meeting. Batt pointedly looked at his watch and asked why I was late. I told him I'd been too busy being a someone's servant instead of a master. Batt laughed and drove on.

But woe be to the staff member who was rude to someone who had taken the time to come to the governor's office. Even the guy who kept writing about the transistors the aliens had put in his tooth fillings got a polite letter of response every single time.

Batt monitored state government through regularly-scheduled meetings with groups of agency heads, and by reading end-of-week memos prepared by staff members who reported about what was going on at their assigned agencies. He had a first-rate scheduling assistant, Eva Gay Yost, who juggled his time to best advantage. And to the extent possible, he had an open-door policy when he was in the office. Staff members with questions to ask or SIMIs to take care of only had to rap on his door frame, and if he was free, he would motion us in.

Beyond that, he announced early on that he intended to visit in person with employees at every state agency. Over a period of several weeks, Eva Gay matched the governor's time with agencies' preferences. The visits were open-ended—that is, he had no set agenda, but rather spent his time listening to and answering questions from state employees. The accompanying staff member took notes on the issues that needed follow-up. Even now, years later, I still meet state workers, retired or still active, who remember his visit, some saying it was the only time they remember a governor visiting in person.

I mentioned Batt's temper. I ought to know. I did something that made him angry. That happened late in the week one week. He didn't want to ruin my weekend, so he waited until Monday morning, buzzed me on the intercom, asked me to come to his office. Once I was seated, he shut all the doors, which was a clue to me that things weren't going well. Then he let me have it. It was awful. I thought I was about to lose my job.

And when it was over, it was completely over. He never mentioned it again. He had the rare ability to speak his piece and then put it behind him. I also know of times that he sent hand-written notes of apology when he thought he'd been unfair or unkind to someone.

Batt is not a black-and-white kind of guy: he really looks at all sides of an issue. One of his signature achievements was getting legislative approval to extend workers compensation to agricultural workers. On the day he signed the legislation, I congratulated him for pushing the bill through. He was oddly somber about his success. He said he'd lost friends over the issue, fellow farmers who worked hard and had difficulty making ends meet in bad years. He'd listened to their objections, yet still thought this was the right thing to do. But winning on that issue was not an occasion for celebration as far as he was concerned.

Of course, the hot issue of his first year was the problem of nuclear waste storage in eastern Idaho. Batt signed an agreement outlining what Idaho would and would not do, and almost immediately encountered opposition. One of the vocal opponents was actor Bruce Willis, who said he would see Batt and others working at 7-Eleven stores unless the agreement was rescinded. If memory serves, a few 7-Eleven store managers sent job application forms to Batt.

In the end, opponents collected enough signatures to put an initiative on the general election ballot in 1996. It basically would have voided Batt's agreement and required any future agreement to be approved by voters. I mentioned to the governor that it seemed to be a wildly popular initiative. Batt, who was taking every chance to talk to the public about what the agreement did and why it was important, told me not to worry. He predicted he would get a two-thirds "no" vote come election day.

As it turned out, 62.5% of the voters rejected the initiative. I teased the governor about falling short of his 67% goal. Well, he said, if he'd just had one more week . . .

Batt had pretty good relations with reporters during his term. True, he liked to point out what he considered any unfair or inaccurate reporting. He took me with him once when he hustled down to the press section of the statehouse to point out to the reporter that he'd used "peek" instead of "peak," or vice versa. Batt was also a stickler for good grammar and a letter with a grammatical error got a big SIMI and an on-the-spot English lesson.

But I think Batt identified with reporters: he had written newspaper columns in the past and continued writing throughout his term in office whenever he had something important to say. He also wrote poems, music, notes, and so on. But as far as I'm concerned, his best piece was a poem he wrote honoring the ninety-one miners who lost their lives in the Sunshine Mine Disaster of 1972. He didn't show it to me; I saw it on a plaque in the statehouse, near a statue of a miner. My favorite verse is this:

We are loggers

We are your neighbors
We share the high country with you

But we sing our song
To the buzzing of the chainsaw
And do our dance on the spinning logs

There's no room in the mine
For our trees to fall
But we are Idahoans
And we were miners then.

During Batt's term, north Idaho experienced awful floods. Batt visited the area, mainly to show residents that he knew what was happening to them and that state government cared about their difficulties. One woman stood with the governor as they watched her house—still not paid for—float by, and she later told me he hugged her while she sobbed and sobbed.

The flooding was so bad that then-president Bill Clinton flew to Idaho and held a meeting with state officials at Gowen Field in Boise. Batt went to the meeting, and when he returned to the office, I asked him how it went. Fine, he said, because the president was doing what he was best at: "Feeling my pain and spending our taxpayer dollars." Then, the smart-alec answer aside, he commented about Clinton's warm and friendly personality.

Soon after, Batt and I flew to New York for that year's educational summit. Batt being Batt, we flew economy, and the governor spent most of the flight working crossword puzzles. (He once showed me his secret for getting through boring meetings: he stashed crosswords in the backs of his notebooks.) The meeting was held at the IBM campus, a beautiful facility where staff members were free to wander while governors were in meetings. All that changed on the day that President Clinton was to appear. Suddenly, there were bomb-sniffing dogs everywhere, large windows were covered up, men in suits checked name tags and directed us on where to go. The governors were seated in a large auditorium, Batt right in the middle. Clinton, on stage, spotted Batt in the audience, shouted out his name, and waved—the only governor singled out. Batt beamed.

Flying economy was just one of the ways Batt was careful about spending the public's money. His own money was a different matter. Once he read a letter from a grandmother worried about the cost of enrolling her grandson for his senior year in high school. I got the SIMI and called the school to ask about the kid. The principal assured me that the school had already given the young man part-time work around the school so he could earn enough for his activity fees, locker fees, letter jacket, and so on. I reported back to Batt that the situation was all taken care of. But he went one step farther, and sent the kid a personal check, along with a handwritten note telling him to use the money to buy some new clothes for his senior year. And he made it clear that the money was a gift, not a loan.

Things didn't always go smoothly, of course. At one point some group – I honestly don't remember who they were or what they wanted – announced ahead of time that they were going to go to the governor's office and make a citizens' arrest. They were all milling around in the reception area when Batt strode out of his office, glared up at the big, burly visitors, and asked them just what they planned to do with him. They were speechless. After a moment, Batt announced, "Well, I've got work to do," turned on his heels and went back into his office. Thus ended the great citizen confrontation.

Batt was, and is, is a strong human rights advocate. He has often credited his mother and his military experience for opening his eyes to human rights injustices. So, it wasn't surprising that he was invited to speak to the Kootenai County Task Force on Human Rights, then coping with the Aryan Nation, about human rights issues. Batt wrote a dramatic speech that began with two rhetorical questions: "Where is Sid Dunagan's grandson? Where is Jack McGoldrick?" (Both men died during WWII; Batt wanted to make a point about the sacrifices made for freedom.) Batt told me later he was nervous that someone who had had a few too many pre-dinner cocktails might shout out "I don't know! They were here a minute ago."

Towards the end of his term, I asked Batt what had surprised him most about being governor. He said he'd thought he knew a lot about state government, given his years in the Idaho legislature and on the Board of Transportation, but found out there was a lot more to learn. The big surprise, he added, was that people he met expected him to be knowledgeable about pretty much everything in state government *and* to have an opinion on those things.

The best thing? "I'm never late to a meeting because those meetings don't start until I get there," Batt wisecracked. "Also, I get a reserved parking spot."

Wisecracking aside, Batt was proud of being a steady hand at the wheel of state government and of using his position to improve the lives of all of Idaho's citizens. Years later, someone asked me to come up with one word to describe Batt's tenure. I picked "housekeeper." I don't think Batt much liked that description, but what I was trying to say was that he left the state a better place for his leadership: budget balanced, work force trimmed and efficient, large problems solved, state's reputation improved.

Those of us on his staff were fortunate to work for someone whose judgment we respected and admired, someone who never abused our trust. At the end, when we were compiling our memories of those four years, Jeremy Pisca, one of the younger staff members, wrote that if he had the last dollar on earth, he would feel comfortable turning it over to Batt for safe keeping. The rest of us knew exactly what Jeremy meant.

Governor Batt served only one four-year term. He cited his age and his other interests for deciding not to run again. Still, to this day, he hosts luncheons a couple of times a year, always at Yen Ching, to gather together those of us who worked for him so long ago. It's a mark of our affection for him that those of us who are still around always make time for those reunions.

Second time's the charm - Batt on the campaign trail for governor in 1994. *Photo courtesy of the Idaho State Archives.*

Gubernatorial candidates Phil Batt (left) and Larry Echohawk (right) at a 1994 debate in Coeur d'Alene. Rod Gramer (center) is the moderator.

Four former Idaho Governors celebrate the inauguration of Governor Phil Batt (left to right) Governors Cecil Andrus, Don Samuelson, Phil Batt, Robert Smylie, John Evans. *Photo courtesy of the Idaho State Archives.*

Governor Batt kept his promise to meet regularly with Idaho Tribal leaders. *Photo courtesy of the Idaho State Archives.*

Phil Batt jamming with guitar great Chet Atkins at Governor Batt's 1995 Inauguration Ball.

Governor Batt on the clarinet jamming at his Inaugural Ball with his friend jazz great Gene Harris. *Photo courtesy of the Idaho State Archives.*

Governor Batt signing landmark nuclear waste agreement with U.S. Energy Secretary Bill Richardson and (left to right) Senator Dirk Kempthorne, Idaho House Speaker Mike Simpson and Congressman Mike Crapo looking on. *Photo courtesy of the Idaho State Archives.*

Governors Cecil Andrus and Phil Batt at the Governor's Cup fundraiser to raise scholarships for students.

Christmas card from Phil and Francee Batt.

(Left to right) Francee Reilly Batt, Governor Batt, Eva Gay Yost.

Governor Batt, wife Francee and the governor's golden retriever Sully.

RANDY STAPILUS is a long-time writer of Idaho politics and history, and is the author of a number of books on Idaho. He was a reporter and editor at newspapers in Coeur d'Alene, Lewiston, Boise, Caldwell and Pocatello, and for many years has written a regional column on politics and government. He lives in Carlton, Oregon.

Photo courtesy of Randy Stapilus.

Randy Stapilus

Phil Batt was the first state legislator I ever interviewed. That was more than four decades ago, and I was a freshman student at the University of Idaho and a new reporter for the college newspaper, the Argonaut. One day some policy issue involving the university - I've long since forgotten what it was, though it seemed contentious enough at the time - came up. It was my job to place a phone call to a legislator who was directly connected to it.

That legislator was Phil Batt, then a legislative veteran and majority leader of the Idaho Senate, a smart, crisp, and highly respected figure at the Statehouse, and helpfully a UI alum. I was a little concerned about whether this eminent - even then - figure in state government even would bother to pick up the phone for me or provide any useful information if he did.

No worries: He did both. He got back to me quickly, and he was an easy but concise, informative, and clear interview, friendly and displaying, even at that distance to someone he didn't know, a sense of humor. I don't remember any of the subject matter, which wasn't of lasting importance. I do remember him.

What's remarkable to me is how little my impression of him has changed in all these years, ever since that phone call.

In the years (decades?) to come, I interviewed Batt - and just talked with him - many times, through his years as a legislator and candidate for state office and up into his time as governor, the latter of which was too short a stretch. (I thought then as I do now that the one term he served was half as many as there should have been.)

That first phone call in the mid-70's was a good primer in what to expect as I interacted with Phil Batt over the years to come, and what a lot of people experienced, and in the qualities that set him apart from most other people in politics (or elsewhere). I have viewed him from the perspective of a journalist and simply an observer at a distance; but I have talked to many people over the years who saw him from other angles - employer, colleague, political competitor or otherwise - and their views of the type of man he is seldom have much differed from each other or from mine.

The qualities we've all seen weren't necessarily unique to him, but they were strongly expressed, and they interacted in his personality in useful ways.

More than most political people, he has in combination a sense of humanity, practicality, respect for other people and an ability and seemingly eager willingness to learn.

His humanity found some expression in his sense of humor, which seldom seemed far from the surface.

I noticed it first in his office at the state Senate, where for some years he kept a talking bird. It never failed to amuse everyone in the area, especially when it engaged in its habit of repeating snippets of Statehouse conversation.

But there was much more. Such as the notes Batt often would dash out from the presiding chair in the Senate to reporters like me sitting nearby, always signed with a scrawled image of a bat. (Batt sent out lots of notes.)

Or his trademark campaign "Battmobile."

Batt's public manner could come across as crisp and stern, but people who spent time around him had a far more rounded sense of his personality.

That found expression in the way he treated people, with straight-forward respect, which led to a lot of very long-term loyalty, extended in both directions.

It even found expression in his musicality, such as when he occasionally joined Gene Harris for an evening playing jazz at the old Idanha Hotel.

More publicly, Batt's humanity showed in his official policy, such as in his work on civil rights legislation (he helped create the state Human Rights Commission), which was not subject matter his home district was necessarily clamoring for. But all of those things were just a few facets of the humane perspective he carried.

One of his newspaper columns from 1975 offered this: "Of all mankind's baser modes of behavior, I believe that racism is the worst. It is the prime cause of a majority of wars. It causes fist fights, murder, and fear. Perhaps worse, it causes millions of people to live in degradation and hopelessness."

That suggests a breadth of world view, an insight into the way his mind works. Phil Batt may have counted himself a conservative, but simple recitation of dogma has never been his approach.

Phil Batt is also a practical man, whether in business or government. He is principled and knows about goal setting and aspiration, but vague ideologies, the bane of so much of American politics, seem to have found less purchase on him than on many in politics. Results matter, and they, rather than a simplistic "that's my philosophy," give him grounding. (Why is racism a bad thing? Batt's statement brings it home concretely: conflict, war, degradation.)

His humanity also lets him see the human being in people generally, including and maybe especially in those who opposed him.

Batt was a partisan political figure, to be sure. He ran under the banner of the Republican Party, led members of it in the legislature, chaired the Idaho Republican Party and led its ticket in races for governor. There was nothing wishy-washy about his loyalties.

He was a natural enough leader in the legislature that he spent many of his terms in the Senate (he was in and out of the legislature several times over the years) as a leader. As party chairman he may have been the single most effective party chair - of any party - in Idaho history, taking an organization battered in the 1990 Idaho elections and, by the election of 1992, turning it into an organization so powerfully effective it has not relinquished commanding majorities in Idaho politics in all the years since.

He was a leading political adversary of Idaho Democrats, but never was he their enemy: He approached them not as an evil force to be eliminated, but as a loyal opposition whose ideas just weren't quite as good as those on his side. He has had many friends through many years in the opposing party - Democratic Governor Cecil Andrus, for one - and widespread respect as well.

When people talk about the more cooperative politics of yesteryear, Phil Batt is one of the practitioners they're talking about.

Batt's is a view of politics and the world not so rare years ago, though Batt exemplified it better than many; but it has become scarcer and precious in the years since.

He approached his service in government with another quality, too: A willingness to learn.

That's really uncommon, especially among political people who have spent a long time in and around office. By the time Batt became governor he had experience in state government, in the legislature and working in and around the executive branch, reaching back 30 years.

He might have been forgiven if, after all that, he had figured he simply knew it all and could act accordingly - that being a mistake many others in many places have made.

Batt did not make that mistake. He had studied and learned in the years before he became governor, but he did not stop then. He did not reach for cheap, easy conclusions, and even after announcing that he would not seek a second term, he kept on learning about the state and the work of its government.

Another governor might well have ordered the execution of Donald Paradis, who had been convicted of first-degree murder. The crime was heinous, and Batt was not an automatic opponent of the death penalty. Nevertheless, faced with the decision of what to do about his case, Batt recalled in his memoir, "I cancelled a week of appointments and devoted my entire attention to the matter."

The easy thing to do - as a matter of politics - would have been to let the execution proceed. Instead, Batt weighed the evidence and found enough doubt to block that punishment. It could have been that we'd never know for sure whether that action was justified, but in fact we do know: Another prisoner later pleaded guilty to the murder, and Paradis was exonerated.

You could see some of the same willingness to swim against the current when Batt formed his "Committee of One" - himself - to investigate the consequences of the "lock 'em up" mentality in state corrections. He pushed for improvements, but the tide in the other direction was strong then.

Idaho has needed in the years since more public officials willing to tackle what Batt was trying to wrestle with more than two decades ago.

The world is not a simple place, and Batt has never seemed to treat it as such. People are not abstractions to him: They are living beings worthy of respect.

We could use more leaders like that now.

More citizens like that, too.

DR. JIM WEATHERBY was the director of the Public Policy Center at Boise State University, director of the Social Science Research Center, and an associate professor for the Department of Public Policy and Administration until his retirement in 2006. Weatherby was also the executive director of the Idaho Association of Cities. He has appeared frequently on Idaho Public Television and KTVB-TV providing political commentary. In 2019, Weatherby received the Ed and Dottie Simpson Award for Civic Engagement from the Boise City Club. The award recognizes an individual who embraces the idea that no problem is so great that it cannot be solved by people with open minds and civil discourse. Dr. Weatherby is also co-author of Th*e Urban West: Managing Growth and Decline* and *Governing Idaho: Politics, People, and Power*, which he wrote with Randy Stapilus.

Jim Weatherby was honored with the Stimpson Award for Civic Engagement by the City Club of Boise on Wednesday, Nov. 13, 2019 at JUMP. Photo courtesy of Betsy Russell/Idaho Press.

Jim Weatherby

I first met Phil Batt while I was with the Association of Idaho Cities (AIC) in the mid 1970s. Batt was the Senate majority leader and I was in my first session as a lobbyist for the AIC from 1974 to 1989. I was also involved in technical assistance, research and training programs for cities throughout the state providing me with opportunities to observe hundreds of elected officials, their style, competence and character.

ACKNOWLEDGES A CLOSE CALL

I don't remember having much contact with Batt during what was my first year of lobbying but I know we disagreed on AIC's top legislative priority: local option taxation for cities, House Bill 80. HB 80 had successfully passed first through the House, and then the Senate's Local Government and Taxation Committee. It was a herculean lobbying effort: the Committee was to be sarcastically renamed "The Senate Good Government and No Taxation Committee" for its very negative view of most tax or fee increases.

HB 80 was reported out of committee to the amending order supposedly for some technical changes. Unfortunately for cities, the only amendment to the bill was to strike the enacting clause which killed the bill and which didn't require a roll call vote.

Senator Batt later acknowledged that if the bill had a roll call vote, it would have probably passed and been signed into law by then Governor Cecil Andrus who supported local option.

A RENAISSANCE MAN

Prior to becoming governor, Batt had spent over 30 years in politics making him one of the most experienced candidates for statewide office in Idaho history. He was rarely, if ever, criticized as being a "career politician". Batt found many ways to serve: state representative, state senator, lieutenant governor, Republican state chair, and governor and had many interests beyond government and politics. Jazz clarinet, fishing and gardening likely provided a sometimes much needed respite. His other job of onion and hops farmer gave him the unique perspective of "big" government vs the common folk.

FILLING THE SEATS

Hard to believe today, but in 1990 the Idaho Republican party was in trouble. Their losses were historic. You have to go back to 1958 to find a worse election result. Republicans held only half of the Senate, lost both seats in Congress and three statewide offices. The Democratic governor, Cecil Andrus, had won a landslide reelection in 1990. The victory gave Democrats control of the governorship for another 4 years making it 24 consecutive years that a Democrat sat behind the governor's desk.

In 1992 Batt became chair of the Republican party. He toured the state focusing on his job of bringing Republicans back together. It was obvious that Cecil Andrus had won reelection with not only support from Democrats and Independents but also with moderate Republican votes. As Batt recalled, "I toured the state for months, organizing, organizing. Our appeal was that we welcomed all as long as they wanted limited, economical government. We filed for nearly every spot. We won big time and we have won ever since."

Batt could honestly take credit for a big win especially in legislative races. When he became Chair the seats in the Idaho Senate were tied 50% to 50%. After the 1994 election, the percentages were 23% for the Democrats to 77% for the Republicans. The picture in the House was not any rosier for the Democrats. Democrats occupied only 19% of the seats to Republicans 81%. Now dominated again by Republicans, it was one of the most Republican legislatures in the country.

Batt could also take much credit for his own gubernatorial victory over Attorney General Larry EchoHawk who was also a strong candidate — no also-ran. In fact, much of the national and international media eagerly talked about the possibility of the election of the first Native American governor in the United States overshadowing Batt's campaign which made his win even more impressive.

THE COMMON MAN

Over the years, I've observed politicians do some interesting things. One in particular happened at the Associated Taxpayers Conference in late 1994 just days before the legislature organizing session. The conference had become a very popular event at the Boise Centre on the Grove in the Summit Room that has steeply tiered seating and the main doors are at the front of the room. Attendance numbered in the hundreds and ranged from local and state elected officials, lobbyists and business interests. That year, the featured speaker was Governor-Elect Phil Batt. He arrived early for his presentation and unexpectedly discovered standing room only. Apparently not wanting to create a distraction in finding a seat and interrupting the speaker, Batt just sat down on the stairs awaiting his turn. Yes, he did, and it tells as much about this extraordinarily down-to-earth individual as could any other example. Talk about being comfortable in your own skin.

UNFORCED ERRORS

In his first week in the governor's office, Batt became embroiled in two major controversies.

Idaho's governor appoints agency boards and commission members; agency directors are primarily appointed by the individual board or commission. At the end of a commissioner's term when the current governor is able to appoint a new commissioner or board member, that board in turn appoints the director, and the agency might then shift direction through this indirect influence of the governor. The director of the Fish and Game Commission is one that does not serve at the pleasure of the governor but legally serves at the pleasure of the Commission.

Batt asked for the resignation of all six members of the Fish and

Game Commission because he didn't approve of the direction the Commission was going. The request was unilaterally denied and his attempt to restructure the agency created a storm of protest primarily from Idaho sportsmen. Many were concerned about maintaining the independence of this agency created by Idaho's first initiative enacted in 1938 designed to take partisan politics out of the selection of the Fish and Game Commission director. The director had become controversial in eastern Idaho over some management issues relating to the relocation of wolves and feeding deer during the winter. The Commission was also being accused of arrogance and ignoring constituents' input on policy and management issues. After Batt's effort to secure resignations failed, he did not wait long to admit that his attempt to change the makeup of the Commission was "premature and ill-considered". It was a gutsy move for a new governor to admit a mistake and know when to cut his losses. Overall, the apology probably helped him more than hurt him. People appreciated his candor.

WASTE NOT, WANT NOT

The other early-on major controversy related to the fate of the stored nuclear waste at the Idaho National Laboratory (INL) in eastern Idaho near Idaho Falls. Batt's handling of the nuclear waste storage issue got him in trouble.

Idaho had banned new shipments of nuclear fuel and the federal government used the national security card in an attempt to lift the ban. The US Navy, concerned because many of its ships and submarines relied on nuclear power, was putting a lot of pressure on the US Department of Energy to strike an agreement with Idaho that would allow storage of nuclear waste at the INL for a certain period of time. Initially, Batt felt that he had no choice but to comply with removing the ban. Eastern Idaho greatly depended upon the INL as a major economic driver so it was imperative that an agreement be reached.

Ultimately, the governor and the federal government struck a deal that Idaho would accept some future shipments but required assurance that all of the waste would be cleaned up and be shipped to a permanent storage site at an agreed upon schedule over a 40 year period or face substantial fines. However, angry constituent-callers didn't approve and the agreement was challenged in the form of a citizens' ballot measure. Their goal was to prevent Idaho from becoming a high level nuclear waste dump especially since the feds had no idea whether or not the permanent repository would ever be opened. Batt's position prevailed on the ballot with over 60 percent supporting the governor's decision. Defending Idaho's interest on this issue was one of the major contributions of Batt's administration providing greater security for the INL and hopefully a clearer path for removing all of the waste from Idaho.

EQUALIZING OPPORTUNITY

Virtually almost all of his adult life Batt has been adamant about improving civil rights protection. So much so, that in 2019 he was awarded the state's top honor, the prestigious Idaho Medal of Achievement.

One specific example of his effort to ensure parity for Idahoans, was the successful passage of legislation for farm workers' compensation. His work on this issue would be one of Batt's crowning achievements, but it came at a real cost. He personally lobbied hard for the legislation to repeal a 79 year old agricultural exemption from the state workers' compensation law. It was a bloody battle between Batt and his once close friends in the agricultural community. To defeat a well-entrenched exemption was a significant accomplishment. Governing Magazine likened the Batt effort to "Idaho's version of Nixon Go's to China". The Wall Street Journal's Dana Milbank labeled Batt as the "Ted Kennedy of the West". No surprise that in Idaho that label didn't stick.

IMAGE BUILDING

Batt committed a lot of time in the last year of his administration to improving Idaho's image. It was a growing realization that the state's extreme right-wingers were getting as much national attention as the state's famous potatoes. That was not good for a state that was increasingly reliant on a growing number of high-tech corporations who wanted to attract the best employees regardless of race, gender or sexual orientation. Batt's campaign to improve Idaho's image was partially based on Idaho's economic self interest encouraging new business to come to Idaho. His campaign found him speaking around the state to numerous organizations highlighting a positive image and hoping his message traveled nationwide. He described his effort as "a committee of one". He celebrated the work of many civil rights groups in Idaho describing what people were doing in various communities (especially in northern Idaho) to counteract the Aryan Nations' influence and other inequities.

As the father of the Human Rights Commission and the defender of the Commission's work, when Batt was senator he conducted several legislative hearings on discrimination issues and in 1969 authored Idaho's first comprehensive civil rights bill. His attention to civil rights issues included a focus on both the Hispanic community and Native American tribes in Idaho. He continues to be active in championing civil rights and has criticized his fellow party members for opposing "Add the Words". "Add the Words" is an LGBTQ2A activist group and political action committee working to add "sexual orientation" and "gender identify" to the state's human rights act.

RIGHTING THE WRONG

Batt's image-improvement campaign included a presentation to the National Association of Schools of Public Affairs and Administration (NASPAA). At Boise State in the Department of Public Policy and Administration we hosted the annual conference of our specialized accrediting body (NASPAA). Several hundred participants, including university leaders of public policy and administration departments throughout the country met in Boise.

In the Spring prior to the October conference, we started getting calls from NASPAA concerned about inquiries they were getting about Idaho's image. The callers had read a very negative article in the New York Times focusing on the state's prejudices. Some of NASPAA members were suggesting that maybe the conference in Boise should be cancelled because of such strong reaction to the negative article. Fortunately, despite this concern, we had a excellent conference with the typical number of hundreds of participants.

One of our featured speakers was Governor Batt who spoke about all of the bad publicity and refuted every major negative critique. It was an impressive presentation and was met with highly positive reviews. The most significant feedback that I can recall was from Joseph Nye, Dean of the Kennedy School of Government at Harvard. He was very impressed with Batt's counter-arguments which offered a clear picture of what was actually happening on the ground in Idaho. There were also many positive comments about the beauty and appeal of Boise. The following year the conference was held in Miami where participants lived through Hurricane Irene. Better to be in Idaho.

NO LITTLE BITE

On more than one occasion, Governor Batt told me how much he appreciated my balanced political commentaries. But he quickly added that most of the time they had "a little bite" to them. Governor, the following is without a "little bite": I haven't always agreed with you on the issues, but to my mind you are among a handful of elected officials who have demonstrated high ethical standards and conscientious attention to the needs and well-being of the citizens of Idaho. Your style, competence and character, is without question of the highest caliber of any and all of Idaho's legendary public servants.

Rod Gramer and Governor Phil Batt following their final conversation on March 5, 2020.

ACKNOWLEDGMENTS

Rod Gramer

Working on a book project starts with an idea but finishes with the help of many people without whose contributions the effort could never succeed. "Lucky" is one of those collaborative efforts. My first thank you must go to Governor Batt who agreed to sit for more than three hours of interviews. This book would not have become a reality without his willingness to reflect back on his life, his 33 years in politics, and on the current political issues facing our state, nation, and world at this critical hour. I also owe a debt of gratitude to Eva Gay Yost, who has served Governor Batt faithfully during both his term as the state's chief executive and after. Eva Gay was my conduit to Governor Batt and my sounding board throughout this project. And I want to thank Governor Batt's wife, Francee, who graciously opened her house for our interviews. Also, I want to thank Jason Kreizenbeck, the governor's long-time aide, friend and protégé who vouched for the worthiness of this project. Each of my interviews with Governor Batt were videotaped by my friend Kristin Shafer who volunteered her time and talents for the project. I want to acknowledge and thank photographer Allan R. Ansell for allowing me to use the wonderful portrait of Governors Batt and Andrus. I think this unique portrait speaks for itself regarding the importance of bipartisan relationships that can be beneficial to the people of Idaho. Of course, I have a huge debt of gratitude to the essayists who wrote such insightful, moving, and heartfelt remembrances of Governor Batt: Governor C.L. "Butch" Otter; Governor Dirk Kempthorne; long-time Batt aide Lindy High; and my pal of 45 years Marc Johnson, who observed Governor Batt both a journalist and as chief of staff to Governor Cecil Andrus. I want to also thank my friends Randy Stapilus, long-time chronicler of Idaho politics, and the incomparable Jim Weatherby, the dean of Idaho political scientists, for contributing essays to this effort. I also owe a huge debt of gratitude to Scott

Gipson, president of Caxton Printers who stopped my sales pitch when I said the book was about Phil Batt. "You had me at hello," Scott said. I want to thank Jocelyn Robertson, book designer, for doing an outstanding job of designing this book. I also owe a debt of gratitude to Janet L. Gallimore, executive director of the Idaho Historical Society and state historical preservation officer, David Matte, State Archives administrator, and Danielle Grundel, photo archivist for providing the wonderful photographs that illustrate Governor Batt's life and political career. Of course, as always, my acknowledgments would not be complete without thanking my wife, Julie, who is my best advisor, editor, and friend. She allows me the space to work on these book projects that send me into my den for solitary hours of research, writing and re-writing. Lastly, I want to thank all the unsung heroes in Idaho who work every day for human rights, equality, and justice, just as Governor Batt did throughout his political career. Their courage helps make our great state a more inclusive, tolerant, equitable and respectful place to live and work. All proceeds of this book will go to the Wassmuth Center for Human Rights where I have the honor of serving on the Board of Directors. Their work is helping all Idahoans, especially the next generation of leaders and citizens, understand how important human rights are to our state's quality of life for all people, not just the few.

Thank you one and all for supporting this project.

Rod Gramer
February 14, 2021

NOTES

1. Phil Batt was born on March 4, 1927. Like many people at the time, he was born at home. Batt's boyhood home was a 900-square-foot farmhouse a few miles from Wilder, in Canyon County. The small house was divided into four rooms—a bedroom for Batt's two sisters, Ruth and Emma, and one for his two brothers, John Jr. and Jim. His parents, John and Elizabeth Karn Batt, had another room of their own, and there was a room for living. The farmhouse had no running water and an outside privy. (*The Compleat Phil Batt, A Kaleidoscope*, copyright Phil Batt, 1999, pages 1-2.)
2. Batt described these workers as "genuine Gypsies" with "moon-and-star-decorated tents, folk dances and fortune-tellers." (Ibid, page 8.)
3. There was a labor shortage in the United States during World War II, so farmers looked outside the country for laborers. The "most reliable" form of labor, Batt recalled, was the Mexican "Bracero Program" (the Mexican Farm Labor Agreement of 1942), which, for the first time, brought Mexican laborers to Idaho. Since then, millions of Mexicans have entered the U.S. to work in agriculture. Many became citizens and, through education and training, have risen to become professionals, farmers and business owners in Idaho. "They are a strong asset to Idaho," according to Batt. (Ibid, page 12.)
4. In 1964, Batt only had a "mild interest in politics." However, his wife, Jacque, had volunteered in Republican politics. Batt decided to "give it a try" and run for his brother, John's seat in the Idaho House of Representatives. (Ibid, page 22.)
5. The 1965 legislature is widely viewed as the greatest legislative body in Idaho history. Lawmakers that year passed several landmark pieces of legislation, including Idaho's

first sales tax dedicated to funding education; reform of the state's judicial system; and, through a special session, the "miserable chore," in Batt's words, of creating the first re-apportionment map of legislative districts in history to meet the U.S. Supreme Court's decision mandating one person, one vote. Several members of the 1965 legislature, including Batt, went on to serve Idaho as governors, U.S. senators and representatives and leaders in business, law and public affairs. (See Appendix 1.)

6. 1982 was a mid-year election and not a good one for the Republican Party. The GOP lost 10 governor seats that year. In Idaho, Democratic governor John Evans was running for a second complete term. (In 1976, then-lieutenant governor Evans assumed the governorship when Cecil Andrus was appointed Secretary of Interior by President Jimmy Carter. Evans won his first full term in 1978, defeating Idaho House Speaker Allan Larsen of Blackfoot.) Batt lost the election to Evans by less than one percent of the vote. Batt has consistently blamed the "Big John" comic book, which depicted Evans as the puppet of union bosses, for his loss. In this conversation, for the first time ever Batt revealed publicly that the political gadfly Ralph Smeed was behind publication of the comic book.
7. 1990 was one of the worst elections for the Idaho Republican Party since the Great Depression. Governor Cecil Andrus, a Democrat, defeated state senator Roger Fairchild in a landslide. The state senate became tied, with twenty-one Republicans and twenty-one Democrats. Democrat Larry Echohawk was elected attorney general and the first American Indian to hold statewide office in Idaho. Richard Stallings was re-elected to Congress from Idaho's Second District, and Boise businessman Larry LaRocco was elected to Congress from Idaho's First District. Only Idaho's two U.S. Senate seats remained in Republican hands. Batt became chair of the GOP at this low point in the party's history. In his own words, he threw himself into the chair's work with "great gusto."

8. By 1994, Idaho's minority-party Democrats had controlled the governorship for nearly a quarter-century, thanks to the popularity of Cecil Andrus and missteps by the dominant Republican Party in 1978 and 1982. Batt decided that he would be the strongest candidate to turn around the GOP's fortunes in 1994, despite being sixty-seven years old at the start of his term if elected. Batt expected state senator John Peavey, a true progressive if there ever was one in Idaho politics, to run against him. Batt's confidence in winning was "severely dented" when Peavey deferred to Attorney General Larry Echohawk, who threw his hat in the ring for governor. Nearly everyone, including Batt himself, expected Echohawk to win the election, and early polls showed that to be the case. Echohawk's campaign drew a great deal of national attention because, if elected, Echohawk would be the first American Indian governor in United States history. As it turned out, 1994 was one of the worst election years in history for the Democrats, thanks in no small part to the unpopularity of President Bill Clinton. Echohawk's celebrity outside the state didn't help his chances, either, as Idahoans are always suspicious of outside influence. Batt also benefited from the strong, grassroots Republican organization he had built as party chair. (Ibid, page 30-31, and the author's own analysis as a journalist who covered this race at the time and moderated one of the debates between Batt and Echohawk.)
9. The controversy over radioactive waste at what is now called the Idaho National Laboratory in eastern Idaho is a complicated one. For those unfamiliar with Idaho, it might be surprising that in the late 1940s, Admiral Hyman Rickover selected the eastern Idaho desert as the location for the birth of the country's nuclear navy. The federal nuclear research facility that bloomed on an 893-acre reservation in the Idaho desert also became the birthplace of nuclear power. The nuclear propulsion for the world's first nuclear submarine, Nautilus, was developed at the Idaho site. The first nuclear-generated lightbulb was lit in the nearby city of

Arco. Idaho has benefited economically for years from the federal government's decision to locate its research laboratory in eastern Idaho. But the downside has been the large quantity of radioactive waste generated from the work at the site, and also the radioactive waste that has been transported into Idaho from other waste-generating sites, including from the Three Mile Island nuclear reactor accident in Pennsylvania. In the 1970s, while reporting for *The Idaho Statesman*, my colleague Lonny Rosenfeld and I broke the story about the federal government pouring radioactive waste through an open injection well right into the Snake River Aquifer, one of the most valuable subterranean water sources in the United States, and essential to irrigators along the Snake River Plain. Our stories created a firestorm of opposition and put a spotlight on the waste stored at the federal facility. A series of governors, including four-term governor Cecil Andrus, had been unsuccessful in getting the federal government to remove the existing waste and stop new waste from entering the state. Andrus had battled the federal government for most of his political career, starting during his first gubernatorial term in 1971. His frustration in not getting the waste removed hit a boiling point in the late 1980s. He started looking for an opportunity to have a confrontation with the U.S. Department of Energy, and for a way to dramatize the seriousness of the issue. His opportunity came in 1988 when the Department of Energy shipped a load of waste from its Rocky Flats arsenal near Denver by rail to Idaho, despite a governor's order that no new waste enter the state. This was the opportunity Andrus needed to make a dramatic point. A train carrying a load of the Rocky Flats waste had been stopped in Blackfoot, Idaho, several miles short of the federal nuclear research facility. Not trusting the federal government, Andrus ordered the state police to put a state trooper on duty to guard the waste twenty-four hours a day as long as it was in Idaho. Andrus got the attention he wanted when a photographer for *The New York Times* took a picture of a muscular state trooper standing guard, giving the impression that the squad car was actually blocking the train's progress to the nuclear waste site. The next day the picture ran above the fold on the front page of the *Times*. Soon national TV reporters were scurrying to Boise to interview Andrus, who even hinted he might dispatch an Idaho National Guard tank to the area if the federal government didn't send the waste back to Colorado. The stunt got the attention of the U.S. Department of Energy, which summarily sent the train back. (*Cecil Andrus: Politics Western Style*. Sasquatch Books, 1998, by Cecil Andrus and Joel Connelly, pp. 156 and 157.)

10. Unfortunately for Idaho, the nuclear waste issue was not resolved by the time Andrus' fourth term ended in 1995. Andrus had, however, taken the federal government to court and new shipments of waste were held in limbo until that lawsuit was settled. At that point, the waste issue fell into the lap of Idaho's newly-elected governor, Phil Batt. There are two different versions of what came next. In his memoir, *Cecil Andrus: Politics Western Style*, Andrus wrote that as he was leaving office, he "quietly encouraged" Batt as the new governor was working on a comprehensive agreement with the federal government to resolve the issue (p. 204). But Batt insisted in my interview that Andrus had never prepared him for the "terrible jolt" he got when he took office and had to deal with the nuclear waste issue. Batt was in office less than two weeks when Admiral Bruce DeMars flew to Boise on a navy jet and told Batt that Idaho's blockage of spent fuel rods from the aircraft carrier Nimitz would put the carrier out of commission. Furthermore, according to Batt, members of Idaho's congressional delegation, including Senators Dirk Kempthorne and Larry Craig, informed him Congress probably would force Idaho to accept the waste. That's when Batt decided to negotiate a settlement that would get the waste out of Idaho and resolve the stalemate with the U.S. Navy. During a critical meeting in Minneapolis with DeMars, the navy was still adamant about making the waste shipments to Idaho and were reluc-

tant to make commitments about removing the waste. Even though Batt was being pressured by Idaho's congressional delegation to make a deal, he walked out and told DeMars he would see the navy in court. "It was then that they came forward with most of the concessions," Batt recalled. "After further meetings, I was able to obtain the stipulations" that ultimately ended up in an agreement. (Ibid, p. 42.)

Andrus initially criticized the agreement because he didn't think it was as strong as it could have been. He was especially critical over the way the federal government would be fined if it didn't achieve its mandated timetable for removing the waste. Eventually, Andrus supported Batt's deal. In his memoir published in 1998, Andrus wrote, "The deal negotiated by Phil Batt was better than no deal at all." (Ibid, p. 206.) A year later, Batt published his own memoir and reacted to Andrus' criticism. "I must tell my friend Cecil that I got every ounce of flesh that I could get. If the navy had not been in a bind, we could not have come close to the deal we made." (Ibid, p. 44.)

As it turned out, Andrus and Batt formed a strong alliance in an effort to hold the Department of Energy's feet to the fire and live up to the terms of the negotiated agreement. That alliance lasted from 1995 until Andrus' death in August of 2017—some twenty-two years. During my interview with Batt in the winter of 2019, he predicted that Idaho's current generation of state leaders would renegotiate the agreement after his death. As it turned out, they renegotiated the agreement nine months after Batt made that prediction, and while he was still very much alive.

11. On November 6, 2019, Governor Brad Little and Attorney General Lawrence Wasden announced that they had renegotiated part of Governor Batt's agreement with the federal government. Here is the way Little and Wasden announced the agreement:

Boise, Idaho) – Governor Brad Little and Attorney General Lawrence Wasden have reached an agreement with the U.S. Department of Energy that provides a path to resolve the department's breaches of the state's 1995 Settlement Agreement and re-commence research on commercial spent nuclear fuel at Idaho National Laboratory (INL).

Despite success on the part of the Department of Energy to achieve significant cleanup milestones since 1995, breaches started in 2012 when the department failed to meet a commitment for treating sodium bearing liquid high level waste at INL. The department later fell behind on shipments of transuranic waste from INL to its Waste Isolation Pilot Plant in New Mexico and ultimately missed a 2018 deadline for all such waste to be out of Idaho. As a result of these breaches, the State of Idaho invoked its remedy laid out in the 1995 agreement and blocked shipments of spent nuclear fuel to INL, including small amounts of commercial power spent nuclear fuel intended for research purposes.

Department of Energy officials signed the new agreement earlier this week, and Little and Wasden signed it on November 6. It was carefully and intensely negotiated during most of this year by the Governor and Attorney General and their staff members, along with significant assistance from Congressman Mike Simpson, U.S. Senator Jim Risch, and U.S. Senator Mike Crapo.

The agreement provides a pathway to cure the Department of Energy's breaches by securing clean-up related stipulations that Wasden began pursuing nearly five years ago when the Department of Energy requested to bring commercial research fuel to Idaho, despite being in breach of the 1995 agreement.

Under the framework, INL is granted a one-time waiver to receive 25 commercial power spent nuclear fuel rods – approximately 100 pounds of heavy metal – from the Byron Nuclear

Generating Station in Illinois. Before this can occur, however, the Department of Energy must begin successfully treating sodium bearing liquid high level waste at INL by turning it into a safer dry, solid state. Currently, the liquid waste sits in tanks directly above the Snake River Aquifer, while the Department of Energy works to resolve operational problems at the Integrated Waste Treatment Unit.

The Department of Energy has also pledged to allocate at least 55 percent of all future transuranic waste shipments to New Mexico's Waste Isolation Pilot Plant facility to shipments originating at INL, and to give Idaho priority when additional shipments become available. This allocation will remain in place until all transuranic waste has been shipped out of Idaho. To date, the Department of Energy has shipped more than 31,500 cubic meters of transuranic waste out of Idaho to the Waste Isolation Pilot Plant.

In exchange for the one-time shipment, the Department of Energy also agreed to remove at least 300 pounds of special nuclear material from Idaho by the end of 2021, and agreed to treat at least 165 pounds of Sodium Bonded EBR II Driver Fuel Pins each year until all pins have been treated – no later than the end of 2028.

A second part of the agreement provides that once the Department of Energy has produced 100 canisters of the dry, treated sodium-bearing high level waste, INL may receive additional research quantities of spent nuclear fuel, per a 2011 Memorandum of Agreement between the Department of Energy and the State of Idaho. This can only occur, though, if the high-level waste treatment process is ongoing and the Department of Energy is not in breach of any terms of the 1995 Settlement Agreement.

The agreement only allows commercial spent nuclear fuel to be sent to INL in research quantities and does not allow for the Department of Energy to bring any other type of fuel to Idaho for storage purposes. Any commercial research fuel brought to INL is subject to language in the original 1995 agreement that requires all Department of Energy spent nuclear fuel to be shipped out of Idaho by 2035. The cap on all Department of Energy nuclear waste in Idaho established in the 1995 Settlement Agreement also remains in place.

"This agreement is a significant development in our ongoing efforts to remove legacy nuclear waste from our state while also supporting the essential research mission of INL as the lead national laboratory for nuclear energy research," Governor Little said. "I want to commend Attorney General Lawrence Wasden, Senator Mike Crapo, Senator Jim Risch, Congressman Mike Simpson, Congressman Russ Fulcher, and everyone else who played a role in helping reach this agreement. I also want to recognize the role that former Governors Phil Batt and Cecil Andrus played in securing Idaho's one-of-a-kind agreement back in the 1990s."

"Secretary Rick Perry and the Department of Energy also deserve credit for working with the State of Idaho in good faith to come to this agreement, and for the cleanup successes that have been achieved," Governor Little added. "Idaho is safer and cleaner because of the 1995 Settlement Agreement, and the agreement we executed this week ensures those successes will continue and that the INL will continue to lead the nation and world in energy research and innovation."

"This agreement is good for the State of Idaho," Attorney General Wasden said. "It ensures the Department of Energy's commitment to remove nuclear waste from INL while also incentivizing the department to turn the most dangerous liquid waste into a much safer and more manageable solid. As those who have been familiar with my stance on this issue over the years know, nothing is more important than treating that liquid waste and protecting our precious aquifer."

"I would like to thank Governor Little and his staff for their support through this process," Wasden added. "They've been diligent in their work with Idaho's Congressional delegation and the Department of Energy to get this agreement across the finish line."

In response to the news that Little and Wasden had negotiated a new agreement, Governor Batt issued the following statement:

Statement from Former Governor Phil Batt on New DOE Agreement

"When I was Governor, I signed an agreement between the Idaho National Laboratory (INL) and the State of Idaho. The Idaho National Laboratory was limited in the contract to specific qualification and duties listed on the current document.

I have consistently opposed efforts to modify the pact, because it states INL cannot start on new ventures unless all major provisions and protections to the state have been completed. Several major improvements have not been fulfilled.

Governor Little and Attorney General Wasden have agreed to some changes in the document. Although I did not agree with the changes, nevertheless, I accept them to be Idaho's new agreement with INL.

I have the utmost faith in our Governor and will support him fully. At my age, 92 years old, I will do what I can to help him carry out the new contract. This agreement, now 20 years old, had served us well and resulted in a much better and cleaner site. It is an important part of Idaho. I wish the INL continued success and I know Governor Little will make this a positive step for Idaho." Philip E. Batt

To clarify the record, Governor Batt added this addendum to our interview for this book:

"This interview between Rod Gramer and myself took place over a period of several months. During the first part of the interview we discussed the nuclear waste issue at INL. Since that time, my successors, Governor Little and Attorney General Wasden, have agreed to alter my agreement. My jurisdiction over that matter expired at the end of my governorship twenty years ago. I gave the original part of the interview before the changes to the agreement took place."

12. Batt received many accolades from editorial writers when he announced that he would not seek a second term. "We saw growth. We saw change for the good. He challenged us. He served us. He made Canyon County proud." (*Idaho Press Tribune*, November 1998, ibid, p. 75); the Twin Falls *Times-News* wrote that when Batt was elected, he was viewed as a "transitional" governor. "But Batt has turned out to be anything but a footnote . . . One of the governor's favorite words . . . is honorable. In a political sense, that's a term from another generation, and it speaks volumes about both the man and his vision of his job. . . To act honorably is to follow where the facts and the public interest lead you, whether or not that conclusion fits your ideology and your preconceptions." (Twin Falls *Times News*, June 1996, ibid, p. 75). In the Rexburg *Standard-Journal*, columnist Randy Stapilus wrote that relations between the state and Idaho's five American Indian tribes was "ice-cold" when Batt took office. But Batt turned that into "something approaching

genuine cooperation—no small feat. . . History may treat him better than he thinks." (Rexburg *Standard-Journal*, December 1998; ibid, p. 76.)

13. The only time in his four-year term Batt appealed directly to legislators to support a bill was the issue of workers compensation for farmworkers. His effort was boosted when, during debate over the bill, an uninsured farmworker was injured in an accident. (Ibid, p. 47.)
14. In summing up Batt's four years as governor, in December 1998, *The Idaho Statesman*'s Dan Popkey wrote that Batt's personal engagement on the workers compensation legislation made all the difference. He quoted Batt as saying, "That's the one issue I really did some cranking on. I'd just call 'em in and say, 'Do you think you can help me on this one? I understand the reasons for being reluctant to. And I don't relish making people angry on this, but I think it's something that needs to be done. Can you help me out?'" (*The Idaho Statesman*, December 1998; ibid, p. 80.)
15. For several years, the Idaho legislature refused to extend Medicaid benefits to working Idahoans who made too much money to qualify for the federal health benefits, but not enough to pay for their own health care. In 2018, a coalition of advocates, including Reclaim Idaho, a progressive group pushing for reform in Idaho, received enough signatures to put the issue on the ballot. On November 6, 2018, Idaho voters supported expanding Medicaid to these uninsured Idahoans, sixty-one percent to thirty-nine percent.
16. In June 2008, J. Kirk Sullivan, a long-time Boise business and GOP leader, was defeated for re-election by Norm Semanko.
17. After Batt made these comments in the interview for this book, former congressman and gubernatorial candidate Raul Labrador was elected chair of the Idaho Republican Party on June 29, 2019.
18. Over the issue of breaching the lower Snake River dams to save the wild salmon, Batt said three questions had to be considered: Would removal of the dams or modification

ensure the recovery of the salmon? What would be the economic losses to stakeholders if they were removed? Who would pay for those losses? Batt admitted that the "preponderance of research" indicated that removal of the dams would be helpful, but noted that fish scientists were not in agreement over the long-term benefits. He said the salmon issue "was among the most frustrating and intractable of any I faced in office." (Ibid, pp. 55-57.)

19. Eva Gay Yost is a long-time aide to Governor Batt who still assists him with his affairs in retirement.
20. Terry Reilly was a Democratic state senator from Nampa when he was killed in an airplane crash while campaigning in 1986 to become lieutenant governor of Idaho. Reilly and his wife, Rosie, started Terry Reilly Health Services in 1971, which they ran out of a refurbished house that Reilly called "Gente House" (House of the People). Terry Reilly Health Services has expanded and still provides health care to thousands of under-served citizens in southern Idaho.

APPENDIX 1

The 1965 Idaho Legislature

Many observers of Idaho politics consider the 1965 Legislature the greatest session in the state's history. Arguably its greatest accomplishment was passage with bipartisan support of the state's first sales tax to provide funding for public schools. This act by the 1965 Legislature created what Governor Cecil Andrus used to refer to as the balanced "three-legged stool" that provides stability to Idaho's revenue system, especially for education, the largest state expenditure of them all. Unfortunately, the two other legs of that stool – the property and income taxes – have been undercut by subsequent legislatures, lending less stability and fairness to our overall state and local tax systems.

It is also noteworthy that the 1965 Legislature produced three future governors, Don Samuelson, Cecil Andrus, and Phil Batt, one U.S. Senator, Jim McClure and one member of Congress, Orval Hansen. Here are some of Idaho's political luminaries who served in that Legislature and what they went on to accomplish in their public careers:

House:

Phil Batt, Senate President Pro Tem and Governor

Orval Hansen – 2nd District Congress

William Murphy – Lieutenant Governor

Pete Cenarrusa – House Speaker and Idaho's longest serving Secretary of State

William Lanting – Speaker of the House

Charles McDevitt – Idaho Supreme Court Chief Justice

Bob Huntley – Idaho Supreme Court Justice

Pat Harwood – First President of the Idaho Association of Commerce and Industry

Senate:

Cecil Andrus – Governor and U.S. Secretary of the Interior

Don Samuelson – Governor

James McClure – Congressman and U.S. Senator

Mary Brooks – Director of the U.S. Mint

Harold Ryan – U.S. District Judge

William Drevlow – Lieutenant Governor

Jack Murphy – Lieutenant Governor

Perry Swisher – Newspaper Editor and Idaho Public Utilities Commissioner

Bill Roden – Senate Majority Leader and long-time Idaho lobbyist

APPENDIX 2
Phil Batt's report on his four-year tenure as Governor of Idaho

Governor Batt issued the following assessment of his four years as Governor as he was leaving the Governor's Office at the end of 1998

Four years have gone rapidly by. History will judge what I did or did not accomplish. I believe most public opinion will conclude that I faced problems head on and without equivocation.

I have reduced or eliminated contentious debate on a number of issues. These include:

(1) Nuclear waste. Idaho's agreement is very much in the state's interest but will require forceful guardianship for many years to come. Attached is a full report.

(2) Longstanding disagreements between labor and management have been greatly ameliorated by combining the Department of Labor and Industrial Services with the Department of Employment. Dramatic reductions in employers' taxes have helped to make businesses profitable and to employ more people at higher wages.

(3) Farm workers are covered by Workers' Compensation for the first time. This is a positive improvement. I commend the Idaho Commission on Hispanic Affairs for persevering on this matter. Farmworkers' minimum wage is also a contentious issue which I believe can be settled by negotiation. A much-improved relationship between farmers and employees could result.

(4) Our property tax relief measure, along with the 3 percent cap, have also reduced the intensity of the property tax revolt. The 1 percent initiative is not a matter of contention for the first time in many years.

(5) While many environment battles are still being fought, a better appreciation for opposite views is appearing be-

tween natural resource users and environmental protection groups. Idaho's air and water are improving without large-scale action of fining and shutting down businesses, which inevitably repress job opportunities. New, much tougher mining regulations have been produced by cooperation with both sides.

(6) Passage of HJR6 and HJR8 will not only provide more money for schools. It will also enable the state to get out of some of the no-win arguments regarding cabin sites and other property.

(7) Prison population growth has been blunted by my Committee of One study. My recommendations, adopted by the Legislature, plus a new more realistic attitude in sentencing and parole were overdue and will save taxpayers many millions.

These and other highlights of my administration are included in the packets distributed to you for this meeting.

It has been a high honor and a unique privilege to serve as governor. I leave with some nostalgic regrets but, having served in various capacities for 33 years, I know it is time for me to pursue other interests.

Governor Batt sharing a moment with the first Republican president – the Abraham Lincoln statue is in Boise's Julia Davis Park.